PREDATOR

Dodd leaned up against a telephone pole near the playground of Richmond Elementary School and watched the kids for a while. His attention drifted to a cute blond boy who looked between four and five years old. He was having fun climbing up a solid, stone-covered mound called "the volcano."

There were no adults around, only a few older children playing a short distance away.

After watching him for a few more minutes, Dodd walked over to the little boy and said "Hi." The little boy looked up at him and smiled. Dodd, brimming with confidence, smiled back.

"Would you like to have some fun and make some money?" Dodd asked. The boy seemed unsure at first, but was not frightened. Finally he shook his head no.

"Come on," Dodd urged, still smiling. "This will be fun." When Dodd reached out his hand, the boy took it. They walked together toward the end of the school building, then disappeared around the corner.

It was the last time anyone ever saw the boy alive. His name was Lee Joseph Iseli.

**PINNACLE BOOKS AND *TRUE DETECTIVE* MAGAZINE
TEAM UP TO BRING YOU THE
MOST HORRIFIC TRUE CRIME STORIES!**

BIZARRE MURDERERS   (486-9, $4.95/$5.95)

CELEBRITY MURDERS   (435-4, $4.95/$5.95)

COP KILLERS   (603-9, $4.99/$5.99)

THE CRIMES OF THE RICH AND FAMOUS   (630-6, $4.99/$5.99)

CULT KILLERS   (528-8, $4.95/$5.95)

MEDICAL MURDERERS   (582-2, $4.99/$5.99)

SERIAL MURDERERS   (432-X, $4.95/$5.95)

SPREE KILLERS   (461-3, $4.95/$5.95)

TORTURE KILLERS   (506-7, $4.95/$5.95)

Driven To Kill

GARY C. KING

PINNACLE BOOKS
WINDSOR PUBLISHING CORP.

For the memory of Billy and Cole Neer . . . and
Lee Joseph Iseli.
May their little souls find peace in Heaven.

PINNACLE BOOKS

are published by

Windsor Publishing Corp.
475 Park Avenue South
New York, NY 10016

First Printing: April, 1993

Printed in the United States of America

Acknowledgments

I would like to express my appreciation to Lieutenant C.W. Jensen, Portland, Oregon Police Bureau; Sergeant David Trimble, Detectives Randy O'Toole and Rick Buckner of the Clark County, Washington Sheriff Department, for their cooperation in allowing me to interview them and to study their case files in-depth at my convenience and for providing photographs; to Lee Dane, one of Westley Allan Dodd's defense attorneys, for his candor in assisting my study of Dodd's background; the Vancouver, Washington Police Department; and the Camas, Washington Police Department. Special acknowledgment to William "Ray" Graves, the real hero of the case without whose intervention Dodd might still be roaming the streets, playgrounds, and parks in his hunt for kids.

Much gratitude also to Paul Dinas, executive editor at Pinnacle Books, who had the vision to see the significance and necessity for this book and to see it through to publication. I am also indebted to Rose Mandelsberg-Weiss, Editor-in-Chief at *True Detective* magazine, who persuaded me to tackle this difficult project in the first place.

5

Thanks also to Curtis & Eunice King, my wonderful parents, for their love and for always standing behind me; to Nicolas & Basilisa Engles, for their heartfelt love and support; Joan Moody, my sister-in-law, for helping to keep me on top of the late-breaking news of this case; and to Kevin D. Lundstrom, my lifelong pal who has shown me the meaning and importance of a real and lasting friendship. A very special thank-you to Shar King and Casey Veenendaal for helping to make my life a little bit easier through their kind deeds and unselfish nature. Finally, my gratitude and heart goes out to Teresita, Kirsten, and Sarah for their never-ending support and understanding for my endeavors, without which the completion of projects such as this would be impossible.

Author's Note

The following story about serial child killer Westley Allan Dodd contains graphic depictions of child molestations, sodomy, rape, and murder. Many of the depictions are in Dodd's own words, taken from his nefarious "diary of death," and others were dramatically recreated from nearly three years of interviews with Dodd himself, police officers, and the study of the police case files and psychiatric reports. While these descriptions may be deemed repugnant to some, it was not my intention to offend or to appear gratuitous with regard to the homicidal violence and sex committed against his truly innocent victims. Including these depictions in this book was a tough judgment call on my part, but in the final analysis I decided that it was far more important to include them than to omit them merely for the sake of sparing readers the true horror of Dodd's monstrous crimes. By including the excerpts from Dodd's diary I was able to recreate portions of the story from Dodd's perspective which, I believe, is important to parents, teachers, law enforcement personnel, and psychiatric professionals in gaining a knowledge and better understanding of how the mind of a pedophile and child killer works. By "seeing" a homicidal pedophile in action, a type of "shock" treatment, if you will, we as parents and professionals will hopefully be enlightened and our awareness heightened enough that we can take steps to better protect all of our children, mankind's greatest asset, from other predatory monsters like Dodd. Even though the threat of Westley Allan Dodd has been permanently removed, there are many others like him who are right now trolling our city's parks, schools, playgrounds, theaters, shopping malls, and countless other public places where children can be found, people just like Dodd who are lurking in the shadows and waiting for just the right moment to make the horror start all over again. Hopefully this book will prompt legislators across the country to follow the lead already firmly established by the states of Washington and Oregon to initiate tougher child predator and sex crime laws in their own states.

—G.C.K.

The ugliest of trades have their moments of pleasure. Now, if I were a grave-digger, or even a hangman, there are some people I could work for with a great deal of enjoyment.

— Douglas Jerrold, 1803-1857
Ugly Trades

Life for life,
Eye for eye, tooth for tooth, hand for
hand, foot for foot,
Burning for burning, wound for wound,
stripe for stripe.

— Exodus, XXI, 23

Preface

It was in the late summer of 1989 that a young man named Westley Allan Dodd trespassed into thousands of lives, and before it was over his rampage of unleashed savagery would make it perhaps the most hideously unforgettable summer on record in the Pacific Northwest. The horror he created that summer would, albeit unintentionally on Dodd's part, forever change the way that citizens and lawmakers alike in the states of Washington and Oregon viewed virtually all classes of sex offenders, especially child molesters and child killers.

Dodd, at the time of his arrest, had not yet developed into a full-blown "bona fide" serial killer as set forth in FBI standards, which states in part that for a killer to be classified a serial murderer he must claim three or more victims in at least three separate "incidents." But for all intents and purposes he was a serial killer all right. Dodd fit the mold in that he had claimed two victims in one incident, another in a second incident, and would have committed his fourth murder in a *third* episode if he hadn't been stopped by a screaming child and alert bystanders while he was attempting to carry out the crime.

Although Dodd had not murdered anyone until late that summer, at least not as far as the authorities knew, it would later become crystal clear that this seemingly near-perfect all-American "boy" turned adult had been, in reality, inextricably enmeshed in an extended fantasy state during that period and had been trolling for victims for at least several months before the first murders. He had been gradually working up his nerve to begin the atrocities that would first unbalance the Pacific Northwest, then ultimately shock the rest of the nation.

Powerless, as most serial killers are, in the day-to-day relationships with those whom he closely associated, Dodd had begun searching for someone, not just anyone, but someone special to play out his ultimate power trips on, lurking in the shadows of Portland, Oregon, and Vancouver, Washington, and waiting until the moment to strike was just right. Many people, including psychiatric professionals and police officials, knew about this sex fiend's long history of indecent exposure, child molestation, and violence, but because of the constraints of the system in which they worked they were powerless to stop him from commencing his killing spree.

In many ways, upon retrospect, he was like the monsters that had come before him, killers like Ted Bundy, Jerome Brudos, Dayton Leroy Rogers, the Green River killer, and a seemingly endless slew of other cold-blooded serial murderers who had learned how to manipulate the system. Like his murderous predecessors he sought out complete strangers as his victims. Instead of women, however, the victims of choice of most such murderers, Dodd always preyed upon helpless little children, young boys whose trust he managed to gain with promises of friendship, money, candy, and toys. When it was all over, few could argue that his malignant deeds, perhaps because children were involved, proved more feral and emotionally painful in the eyes of law officers and the disconcerted public than those of his notorious predecessors.

Dodd knew early on that he liked molesting young children, and in his mind the dictum was "the younger the better." He also did what he had to do to avoid jail time, and would play the "game" of the system so that he could continue to molest kids and expose himself. He learned early in his life how to effectively manipulate the system so that he could slip quietly, almost unnoticed, through its cracks. Despite his extensive criminal record as a sex offender in cities and towns throughout the Pacific Northwest, the authorities always seemed to forget about him when he dropped out of a treatment program and moved on to another locale. Because he had been successful at avoiding prosecution for so many of his earlier crimes, Dodd, even at the time of his final arrest, had not significantly changed his *modus operandi*. Under a more sophisticated and more communicative law enforcement system, Dodd's continued criminal activities could have caught the attention of authorities early on and saved the lives of his innocent victims. But the system, even when functioning at its best, had its pitfalls. Thankfully, in response to citizen outrage over his crimes, a superior although controversial system requiring convicted sex offenders to register for the rest of their lives with police agencies is now in place in the states of Washington and Oregon.

If it can be said that anything good came out of this case besides instituting a more efficient system for reporting and keeping track of sex offenders, it is only that this sexual sociopath, clearly a livid monster hiding inside a human shell with an insatiable appetite for violent and bloody death, was stopped before he could put his nightmarish fantasies into full play and snuff out even more young lives. Despite the efforts of four police agencies and numerous detectives to thwart his perverted activities, however, he had committed murder with calculated cold-bloodedness, terrorized entire communities, and virtually turned the populace of two states upside down before being stopped.

There have been few crimes that have instilled such a high degree of fear in a populace as those committed by this killer, mainly because he struck out at pure innocence and left everyone wondering who and where he would strike next. In part by his own design and in part by the laws governing sex offenders that were in place at the time, Dodd ultimately was *driven to kill*.

Prologue

A hushed silence fell over the long, rectangular courtroom when Westley Allan Dodd, flanked by armed sheriff's deputies, appeared through a side door, hands cuffed securely behind his back. After a deputy removed the restraints that held his thin wrists together, the convicted child sex killer took a seat at the defense table next to his attorney. Clad in a light blue, short-sleeved pullover shirt, pre-washed faded blue denim jeans, and a pair of sneakers, Dodd uneasily faced the judge, his back to the families of the victims he'd kidnapped, tortured, and murdered. Their eyes were upon the dark-haired young man, just as they had been throughout the month-long guilt or innocence phase of the trial. They had heard startling, shocking testimony about child molestations, violent depraved sex, torture, and necrophilia.

The courtroom was packed to capacity, and many of the spectators who had sat through portions of the trial had to be turned away at the door. Those who managed to get in were required to pass through a metal detector, just as they had been required to do on all previous days. Everyone present that day, Thursday, July 26, 1990, was there to hear Clark County Superior Court Judge Robert Harris pass sentence on the "normal-looking" pedophile turned child murderer. First, however, Harris had decided to allow members of the victims' families to make public statements.

Karen Osborne, an aunt of four-year-old victim Lee Joseph Iseli, nervously shuffled a sheet of paper as she faced the judge. She was going to read a handwritten statement by Jewel Cornell, the boy's grief-stricken mother. She swallowed hard, looked directly at Dodd for a moment, then began to read from the paper she held with trembling hands in front of her.

"You have taken my whole world apart — my family's world apart," read Osborne from Cornell's emotionally charged statement. "You are the scum of the Earth. You get on the news and the radio and tell everyone how you felt when you did these unspeakable crimes . . . and you get a high just by talking and going over what you did. You make me sick. I hate your guts . . . you are a sick, cruel and ugly person . . . I will never rest until the day your life is taken . . . I hope you rot in hell." If Dodd felt anything as a result of Cornell's statement, he didn't let it show.

Robert Iseli, Lee's father, next stood in front of the courtroom. Brushing back an occasional tear he turned toward Dodd, angrily facing the man who had confessed to brutally raping and murdering his little boy.

"How did we allow *this*," he said, gesturing toward Dodd, "to end up where he is today? It is sad to take a life. . . . Taking a life, any life, even this man's, is never right. It is a grave decision that the state has to make. . . . So do we blame ourselves for this death? No. We are left with no choice."

Relatives of the other murder victims—Cole Neer, eleven, and his brother, Billy Neer, ten—declined to make a public statement.

"Do you have a statement to make before this court, Mr. Dodd?" asked Judge Harris.

"Yes, your honor," said Dodd as he stood up at the defense table. "I didn't offer any mitigating evidence during the penalty phase because, in my mind, that's just an excuse. And I don't want to make any excuses."

Dodd occasionally looked up at the judge and stoically reiterated how he had been arrested numerous times over the course of his life for sex crimes against children, and stated matter-of-factly how the criminal justice system had failed him and his victims.

"I do not blame the criminal justice system for anything . . . but the system does not work and I can tell them why. . . . It doesn't really matter why the crimes happened. I should be punished to the full extent of the law, as should all sex offenders and murderers . . . I can accept a death sentence, and I don't want to see any delays in carrying it out. . . . If my death will bring peace to the people I've hurt so bad, then it's time for me to die."

"Amen," said someone from the gallery of spectators.

When Dodd finished, Roger Bennett, deputy prosecuting attorney, stepped forward and submitted a legal document to the court that would, if signed by Dodd, allow Dodd to waive his rights to appeal. Bennett fervently recommended that the judge allow Dodd to sign the document.

"I like what Mr. Bennett is saying," Dodd offered. "I don't want this thing tied up in the courts for years." He added that he didn't want the mandatory review of his case by the Washington Supreme Court, and insisted that he did not want anyone filing any appeals on his behalf. He said he would instruct his lawyer to sue anyone who tried to intervene.

"You have an ongoing, depraved, sadistic desire to hurt, injure, and maim others," Harris told Dodd as he looked him square in the eye. "To you, it is clear that murder is the ultimate goal—the ultimate satisfaction . . . I am able to sign your death decree without looking back. . . ."

Chapter One

It was Labor Day, September 4, 1989, a Monday, the last day of summer vacation for most school children from all over the Pacific Northwest. The unbearable heat, as much as holiday tradition, had brought many people outdoors to barbecue and drink beer beneath the slightly cooler shade of the towering Douglas fir trees of the region's many parks and recreational areas. It also had brought out the kids, lots of them, who frolicked carefree under the sweltering sun, naturally oblivious to the oppressive heat, their surroundings, and to the stranger waiting in the shadows who wanted, more than anything else in his life, to do them harm. The last holiday of the summer should have been a day filled with joy and pleasant memories. But it wasn't. Instead, to the citizens of Vancouver, Washington, and much of the region, that particular Labor Day would be remembered as one of the darkest days in the annals of crime history, the day that Westley Allan Dodd, then 28, set into motion his plans to kidnap, rape, torture, and murder little children.

* * *

Dodd's sleepless nights started again two days before Labor Day, on Saturday, September 2, and even though he knew they spelled trouble for him, he didn't care. He couldn't help himself and, when he was alone, couldn't control himself. Something in his innermost psyche was driving his actions now, and before long he knew he would be totally consumed by something he did not understand.

Dodd lay awake much of that Saturday night in the small, hot apartment that he'd just moved into and fantasized about the day that he had been planning for so long. Naked upon his bed, he masturbated fiercely as he recalled several of the previous incidents in which he had molested young children. Afterward, in an entry to the diary he kept, which had become a very special and intimate part of his life, he complained that he had been kept awake most of that night by a stiff erection. He liked erections, to be sure, but only those that succumbed to his fantasies coupled with masturbation. He wasn't at all happy when they lasted all night. He managed to get to sleep only after convincing himself that killing a young boy was the only thing that could satisfy him.

Dodd had actually begun the "hunt," as he would call it, earlier that day after he found Vancouver's David Douglas Park almost by accident. Dodd had only recently moved to Vancouver from the Seattle area, but he spotted David Douglas

Park while driving along Northeast Andresen Road, a busy north-south thoroughfare adjacent to the west side of the park. He was moving some of his things from his dad's house into his apartment when he saw the sign and decided to check it out.

The park was convenient for him, located about a mile northwest of his apartment, and he liked that. It was easy to get to, and its close proximity to his apartment meant that going there frequently wouldn't cut too deeply into his gas money as would, say, going to a park on the other side of town. After he walked through it and visually studied it, he drew a map of the park. He initially noted that the ideal area for carrying out his grim deeds would be along the south and west sides, a densely wooded gully area where the dirt bicycle trails coursed in and out among the trees. But after he became more familiar with the park's layout, Dodd realized that the area he had chosen was distinctly set off and, he thought, perhaps too remote from the rest of the park. The kids that he so desperately wanted might not wander over that far very often, at least not alone. After another walk through the park, during which he again carefully considered the layout, Dodd finally focused his attention on an area that ran east to west. The east end was the most isolated, he saw, yet it was still close enough to the more populous areas from where children would venture off. He found a place near one of the trail heads and sat down on that Saturday evening, where he watched and waited from his inconspicuous vantage point for just the right opportunity to arise.

He waited there from 6:10-6:40 P.M. but saw only three young boys, and they were together. He visualized raping and murdering those boys at the site. He also contemplated kidnapping the boys so that he could "play" with them first, then taunt and humiliate them just as many kids had done to him while he was growing up. To Dodd, the ultimate game was to molest and rape the children, then murder them in the most horrendous ways imaginable. However, for whatever reason, whether he lost his nerve or his conscience took control, Dodd returned home that evening without harming those boys. They were the extremely lucky ones.

Between masturbatory fantasies and napping in the nude, Dodd spent much of that evening preparing a photo album which he labeled, "P—1." It was to fit neatly into his scheme of things, and would eventually become as intimate a souvenir as his diary. He wrote instructions on one of the pages that the following key to the picture sections would apply to when it was finished:

P—photos by other photographers, old and new, some "art."

C—photos of children I see nude, or get

them to pose for me, but I have no sex contact with.

V—photos of children in a more than once (sexual molestation) relationship, whom I trust to keep quiet. Some of these photos may have me in them also.

M—photos of children who I forced, or they cooperated, either way ending in M(urder).

Interestingly, but without benefit of an explanation, several of the "art" photos that Dodd placed in his album were of religious art works that depicted, for example, Mary, Joseph, and the Christ child; the birth of Christ; Virgin and Child; and so forth. He placed behind these religious photos a number of other "art" photographs of nude children. Surprisingly, these photos were not pornographic, at least not to anyone with normal sexual orientation. But the photos that he had cut out from a number of commercially published photography books were very pornographic to Dodd and others like him. To a pedophile, even advertisements that depict children modeling underwear are pornographic.

With the "P" section of photographs now arranged to his liking, Dodd made an entry into his diary in which he wrote that he hoped to begin using video equipment and a Polaroid camera to photograph his child victims of "certain cases" within four months, or whenever he obtained enough money to purchase the necessary equipment. Satisfied that his photo book was now ready for the remaining "C," "V," and "M," sections, he placed it along with his diary inside a briefcase which he slid underneath his bed for safekeeping. He masturbated again and dozed off, but was awakened an hour later by his need for further sexual release. He did not get much sleep that night.

The next morning, Sunday, September 3, after hastily drinking a cup of coffee to revive him from the virtually sleepless night he'd endured, Dodd returned to David Douglas Park where he intended to spend up to five hours to obtain what he so desperately wanted. While he sat and watched, lying in wait like the predator that he was, he again considered whether he would rape and murder his victims at the site or kidnap them and take them to his apartment where he could commit his vile acts and take as much time as he wanted with far less fear of discovery.

"If I can get it home," he had written in his diary prior to leaving, referring to his as yet unfound victim as an object rather than as a person as most serial killers do, "I'll have more time for various types of rape, rather than just one quickie before (the) murder."

He finally decided that he would have to make his choices dependent upon the circumstances at hand on any given day. If a boy was cooperative, he concluded, he might very well take him back to the apartment where he could enjoy him at his leisure. On the other hand, if it became clear that the intended victim was not going to cooperate, he would just have to rape and kill him on the spot as quickly as possible and then get out of there, fast.

By 2:00 P.M. Dodd's prospects of finding a victim again looked slim. He was also hungry. He returned home for lunch, and reflected about the "possibles" he had encountered that day. He jotted down detailed notes, which he would rewrite much more neatly in his diary later so that he could relive at will the fantasies that he had experienced that day in the park.

He hastily scribbled that he had seen two boys earlier that day, about nine and ten years old, who had interested him. The oldest boy had been big for his age—too big, in Dodd's opinion—but the younger of the two had aroused him sexually. He decided that he would have taken the smaller boy to rape and murder, *if* the boy had been alone.

At another point he had watched two girls for a while, estimating their ages to be seven and twelve. He had liked the younger one, and, as before, would have raped and murdered her if she had been alone. But a girl would do only as a last resort. Dodd wanted a boy first and foremost.

He had also seen four boys that afternoon. Three were approximately seven or eight years old, and one was about twelve. As Dodd sat back and watched them, he soon realized that they were looking for a place to urinate. Young boys, Dodd knew, were always looking for a place to "pee" outdoors. Finally one of them had said, "Let's just go for it here," which they did while Dodd watched unnoticed and became excited from his vantage point in the bushes. Dodd had thought that if the older one hadn't been there, he could have easily separated the other three. Once separated he could have murdered the first two quickly and saved the last one, the best-looking of the three, to savor as he raped and murdered him. Under the circumstances, he had decided that it was best not to try anything with that group of boys.

Dodd finished his lunch and his hastily written notes, prepared a cup of tea to go, and resumed the hunt by 2:25 P.M. Over the next hour and a half he considered four boys and two girls, who ranged in age from eight to ten, as victims, but backed away when he saw that they were accompanied by two adult females. Frustrated and angry, he went home at 4:00 P.M. and decided that he should be better equipped for future hunts.

He added long shoe strings and a large Ace bandage to his "hunting gear," which had consisted of only a six-inch fish-fillet knife up to that point. He decided that the Ace bandage could be used to hold the knife to his leg, so that it would "ride better," and he could use the shoe strings for tying up his victims. He realized that he could also use both items to choke his victims, instead of relying on a kid's shirt to strangle his victim like he had previously thought about doing. Besides, he knew that boys often didn't wear shirts in the summer, and it was always possible that one of his intended victims could turn out to be one of those kids who didn't. It was better to have the shoe strings to use as ligatures, he decided, and he would have the Ace bandage as a backup.

Before giving up entirely for the day, Dodd drove to a local Fred Meyer shopping center about three miles from his apartment. The department store was part of a large chain located throughout the Pacific Northwest, and was one that Dodd frequented as much to shop as to watch the kids. It was there that he spotted and was aroused by a six- to seven-year-old boy who was wearing a pair of "cute" shorts, but *no* shirt. A sudden urge to pull the boy's shorts down right there in the store nearly overcame Dodd, but he thought better of it. He'd have been caught for certain, he decided as he left the store and returned to the park one more time. By now he felt compelled, driven nearly to the point of madness to find a victim that he could kill and experience a temporary release from all of the pent-up sexual anguish he had carried for so long.

Dodd had walked approximately fifty yards away from his car when three boys, each about seven years old, passed him on their bikes. He stopped momentarily in his tracks, returned to his

29

car and retrieved his knife. He decided that when the boys returned along the bicycle trail he was going to separate them if he could, murder two of them quickly, and then rape and murder the third one utilizing the stratagem he had already worked out so many times in his mind. But just when he left his car with the knife, they foiled his plans when they turned around and rode away from the park. He returned home again and wondered whether the boys would have stopped if he hadn't gone back to his car for the knife. Now more determined than ever, he vowed to himself to return to the park the next day after deciding that the noon to 3:30 P.M. time frame seemed best. There were more children in the park during that time, and the holiday would surely bring out even more kids.

Dodd awoke at 9:35 A.M. on Monday, September 4, Labor Day. After deciding that he probably wouldn't want to return home before he accomplished his self-imposed mission of death, Dodd packed a lunch to take with him to the park. He also began to reason again that he would be better off to take his victims somewhere else to murder them. If he left murdered children in the park, he decided, he would likely lose his "hunting ground" for up to two or three months. Police would start watching the park, and parents would be afraid to allow their children to go there unaccompanied.

But if the kids just disappeared, he'd be free to return for other victims. Before leaving for the day, he had written in his diary that the park was even better than the river in Richland, Washington, in the eastern part of the state, where he used to molest children and expose himself. He didn't want to do anything that could jeopardize his being able to roam the park safely.

At 1:15 P.M. he spotted two boys, each perhaps nine to ten years old, on their bikes. They stopped along the trail, and Dodd walked past them for a closer look. After passing by he watched them from a distance for a couple of minutes, then walked by them again. As he walked away from them the second time, they followed behind him for a short distance. He became excited when he thought that he had finally found his perfect victims, even if they were a *little* big. In the next instant he turned to confront them, separate them if possible, but they did the unexpected. They turned off onto the fork of another trail and pedaled away from him without looking back.

A couple of hours later a boy, about seven years old, rode his bike past Dodd on the trail. Dodd turned to run after him, to "run him down," he wrote, in his diary later, when he spotted the boy's father a short distance behind. The boy's father, he wrote, "came into view as I saw the boy's great-looking butt on the bike seat." Although again disappointed, Dodd never relented in his hunt for a victim. Today, he somehow knew, was going to be the day.

A few blocks away in a middle-class home located in the 300 block of Council Bluffs Way, two young boys raced for their bicycles, which were parked near the front porch of their house. The boys appeared not to have a care in the world. Their father, who adored them, often wished that he had only one-half of their energy.

"We're going hunting for lost balls!" yelled William Neer, ten, to his father. It was a statement, not a request, part of an almost daily ritual in which William, whom everyone called Billy, and his brother, Cole, eleven, rode their bicycles to a nearby golf course where they hunted for balls that had missed their marks and had gone astray. They nearly always found most of the balls near the driving range, and were paid a penny apiece for them by the golf course's manager. It was easy money for the boys, which they eagerly spent on candy, baseball cards, and toys.

Even though they hadn't lived there long, the McLoughlin Heights neighborhood seemed like a good, safe place to raise children. Automobile traffic, as opposed to some maniac running loose looking for kids to kill, seemed to be a greater concern to parents looking out for their children's safety. It was a few minutes past 4:00 P.M. when the boys left their home, the last time that Clair Neer saw his sons alive.

Being kids, Billy and Cole paid their father little mind as they hopped astride their matching BMX bikes and zoomed off down the street, popping wheelies every half block or so. As always, they arrived at the driving range without a hitch. Excited about the prospect of earning money, they enthusiastically scavenged for the lost golf balls for the next hour and a half.

By 6:15 P.M. Billy and Cole had found all the golf balls they cared to find. They were getting tired and hungry and, after collecting their money, decided that they should head for home. Wanting to arrive home in time for dinner, they took their favorite shortcut through David Douglas Park along one of the secluded dirt bicycle paths, barely a half mile from their house.

Unknown to Billy and Cole, Westley Allan Dodd had begun walking down the same trail only moments before they had turned onto it. Dodd quickly saw them, and deliberately stood in the middle of the trail to force the boys to stop. They were about the age that he wanted, he decided, and there was no one else around. Perfect. He approached them as they looked at him curiously, and instructed them to get off their bikes. Both being obedient kids, they did what they were told.

"I want you two to come with me," said Dodd.

"Why?" asked Billy, sincerely puzzled at the stranger's command.

"Because I told you to," answered Dodd. "You can bring your bikes if you want." Dodd had sensed that Cole was going to leave his bike behind, and he didn't want someone to easily find it and begin looking for its owner. The boys, either out of fear, curiosity, or a feeling that the stranger needed their help, followed Dodd down the path.

Along the way Dodd examined the boys carefully. He realized that their complexion was darker than that of a Caucasian, and he felt like they were of a different race. He had always limited himself to molesting only white children, and had never liked "the idea of (fellating) foreigners." Nonetheless, he was committed. He might not have another chance as good as this for some time.

As they walked along the trail they passed two teenagers at one point. Dodd warned the boys to remain quiet, not to talk to them. Billy and Cole looked at each other quizzically, but obeyed. After the teenagers were out of sight, Dodd asked the boys their names and ages. He was a little disappointed when they told him their ages. They were both older than he had initially thought, certainly older than he liked his boys to be. But there was no turning back now.

They veered off the trail at one point and, following Dodd's instructions, the boys laid their bikes down just off the edge of the path where they couldn't easily be seen. Dodd led them several yards up a hill into the trees and bushes, out of sight of the trail in case someone walked or rode by. He then commanded the boys to stand back-to-back — Billy kept quiet, but Cole kept asking "Why?" at every command — and tied their wrists together tightly, effectively binding the two brothers together with one of the ten-inch shoelaces. Satisfied that neither could get loose, Dodd commanded both of the boys to face him. He then knelt in front of them.

"One of you has to let me pull down your pants," said Dodd as his breathing became more rapid. He noticed that Cole was wearing shorts and Billy was wearing blue jeans.

"Him," said Billy as he looked toward his older brother. Billy, now distraught, began to make whining sounds and was on the verge of tears.

"Why?" asked Cole.

Dodd responded that he wanted to perform oral sex on him.

"Will it hurt?" asked Cole, not fully comprehending what Dodd wanted to do to him.

"No," Dodd replied.

"Okay," said Cole, afraid but wanting to please the man so that he wouldn't hurt him or his brother.

Dodd had been hoping to have Billy since he was younger. And besides, Dodd thought that he was "prettier" than his brother. But he feared that if he forced the issue with Billy, the boy might scream or begin crying louder than the whimpering that he was now doing, and that could spoil everything. So he settled for Cole.

Dodd, now turned on, pushed Cole's button-down shirt up so that he could slide his fingers into the waist of Cole's shorts and underpants, after which he pulled them down to his knees and began to fondle him. Still not satisfied, he performed sex on the boy.

"Why are you doing this to us?" asked Cole.

"Because I have to do it," said Dodd. "I'll let you go in a little bit."

Dodd repeated the process of performing oral sex on Billy, and found himself wanting to do it longer with Billy than he had done with Cole. But as shame and guilt feelings set in as a direct result of the deviant acts being committed against them, Billy and Cole became agitated and even more afraid. Dodd finally stopped, and looked up at Billy.

"I want you to do that to me," Dodd instructed the child. But Billy started crying again, and Dodd was compelled to turn back to Cole.

"You have to do something else," Dodd told Cole.

Both boys, however, told Dodd that they were hungry and that they were late. They had to get home, they said, or else their dad would be angry. To placate them Dodd simply instructed the boys to tell their father that they got lost, even though he knew that neither boy was going to leave the park alive.

Dodd forced both boys to drop to their knees,

and pulled Cole's pants down again. In order to do what he wanted, he realized that he would have to cut the boys loose. He raised his pants leg and removed the knife from its sheath, held in place around the calf of his right leg by his sock, and cut the shoelace that bound the two boys together. Conscious about not leaving behind any evidence that could identify him, he placed the shoelace pieces in one of his pockets. Billy, at that point, offered to go and tell their dad that they would be late.

"You can go in a couple of minutes," Dodd retorted. "I'm almost done." Dodd had Billy lean back onto his heels so that he couldn't make a fast getaway, then returned his attention to Cole.

With Cole's bare buttocks toward him, Dodd unzipped and pulled his jeans and underwear down in the front only, exposing him. Hoping to attain an erection, Dodd began simulating intercourse between the boy's legs from the rear. But, unable to get an erection, he quickly gave up. Dodd, frustrated, made a mental note that he was in too much of a hurry and told himself that he must slow down and relax more next time.

"There's just one more thing," said Dodd as Cole turned to face him. Dodd again took the knife from its sheath. Both boys now faced Dodd in a crouched position about a foot apart, with Dodd centered in front of them. They shrank back in terror when they saw the knife blade in Dodd's clenched hand. He was poised, ready to strike.

"Please don't kill us, mister!" cried Cole. "We won't tell!"

Dodd reached out with the knife and in one swift movement shoved the sharp thin blade deep into Billy's stomach. Dodd, thinking that Billy would drop to the ground, turned to Cole who was now horrified after seeing what Dodd had done to his brother. He started to turn and rise to his feet, but he was too late. Dodd lunged at Cole's stomach, but the blade caught him in the side. By then Billy had grabbed his stomach and had started to run away. Without looking back he headed off in the direction of the sounds of automobile traffic on Andresen Road and to what he perceived as safety. Cole was now down, but he kept moving as he writhed in pain. Dodd nearly panicked. He stabbed him again, and then a third time in the chest. Cole finally lay still.

Fearing that Billy would reach the busy road, Dodd quickly rose and ran after the boy. Both running, Dodd soon caught up with Billy and grabbed him by the right arm.

"I'm sorry! I'm sorry!" cried Billy. As he spun around in Dodd's grip, Dodd stabbed him in the lower side and then again in the left shoulder as he fell to the ground. Dodd didn't stick around to make certain that Billy was dead. Fearing that he would leave fingerprints on the boy's bloody clothes or get some of Billy's blood on himself, he didn't attempt to drag the body into the bushes to

38

conceal it, as Cole's was. Instead, he left Billy right where he had fallen.

The total time Dodd spent with the boys was twenty minutes.

Dodd ran to where the boys had left their bikes on the trail, then walked from that point on to avoid arousing suspicion from anyone who might happen along. He placed the knife back in its sheath and continued on for about thirty yards before deciding to return to Cole's body to make certain that he hadn't left anything behind that could lead the cops to him.

He found Cole flat on his back, his head tilted to the left. His eyes were still open, and his arms lay motionless at his side. He was covered with blood, and Dodd could not discern any signs of movement. At first Dodd thought he saw something protruding from Cole's stomach, but then he realized that Cole's pants were still half way to his knees and what he was looking at were the boy's penis and testicles. Dodd decided that Cole was definitely dead. Finding no incriminating evidence, Dodd considered running back to make certain that Billy was dead, too, but decided not to risk the extra time. Someone, he thought, could come along at any moment.

As Dodd walked away he noticed blood on his left hand. Keeping his hand inside his pocket he calmly walked up the trail to the main park. He greeted an old man and threw a stray baseball back to a couple of young men on the way back to his car. He made every effort to appear as normal as possible to everyone he encountered in the park.

When he got back to his car a few minutes later, Dodd drove out of the park and circled over to Andresen Road. It was there that he saw a man running down the hill toward a convenience store. Dodd figured, correctly, that the man had found Billy and was running to get help.

Dodd wrote in his diary later that he had been pretty shaken up over the incident at David Douglas Park. He thought about it all day on Tuesday, September 5, unable to get his memory's image of Cole's body or Billy's repeated pleas of "I'm sorry" out of his mind. Nonetheless, he managed to report to his job at Pac Paper on schedule. By the time he returned home that day he found that he had calmed down considerably, enough so that he was able to masturbate to his mental images, fantasies really, of Cole and Billy, both when they had still been alive and later, when they were dead and bloody.

Later that evening Dodd wrapped the knife inside an old used manila envelope. He took it to work with him the next day and dropped it into a garbage Dumpster during his lunch hour. The knife, he knew, would never be found.

Chapter Two

Danny Miller*, seventeen, sweated profusely from the sweltering heat of the late afternoon sun as he walked up the steep hill of Northeast Andresen Road at approximately 6:45 P.M. Even though it was Labor Day, he had worked a short shift at a nearby McDonald's restaurant and was on his way home. Five minutes later, at 6:50 P.M., he was nearly halfway to the top. He paused momentarily to catch his breath along the east side of the thoroughfare that ran adjacent to the west side of David Douglas Park. He would have soon made it to the top where Andresen leveled out and intersected with Mill Plain Boulevard if he had not turned onto a trail and headed east into the park to take a shortcut to his home on the other side of the park. It was there on the path that he discovered the seriously injured boy.

At first Miller thought that the human form

The names of some individuals in this book have been changed. An asterisk (*) appears after a fictitious name at the time of its first occurrence.

several yards in front of him was just one of the local drunks, passed out from too much liquor and too much heat. But as he moved closer he saw that it wasn't a drunk man at all. Instead he realized that he was looking at a child, whom he would later learn was Billy Neer. Miller observed that the boy appeared to be of Asian or Native American origin, and couldn't have been more than nine or ten years old.

As Miller called out to the child, he began to wonder what could have happened to him. Despite Miller's attempts to get the child's attention, the boy just lay there motionless in a shallow ditch that ran next to one of the park's dirt bicycle trails. The area, accessible only by foot or by bike, was not clearly visible from the more public areas of the park nor from the other side of the four-lane boulevard. But Miller had been able to see the boy from the point where he turned off by the road's shoulder to take the shortcut through the park, and he ran the rest of the way over to where the boy lay to see if he could help.

He noticed right away that there was blood, lots of it, on the upper part of the youngster's torso and on his legs. Miller's first impression was that the boy had been struck by a passing car, perhaps as he had attempted to cross the busy road, and had been thrown by the impact with the car into the ditch. The boy was unconscious but was breathing, which gave Miller hope that he could be saved. Without moving the boy out of fear of injuring him further, Miller ran as fast as he could toward the nearest telephone, located at a convenience store about three blocks north of the park. Out of breath and in a near panic, he burst into the store and asked the clerk to call 911 for him. When an emergency dispatcher answered, the clerk handed Miller the phone, and he reported what he thought had been a hit-and-run accident.

Lieutenant Roy Brown, assigned to patrol, and a team of officers from the Vancouver Police Department were the first to respond to the 911 call. They arrived at the scene within minutes, as did paramedics from a nearby fire district station. Miller led them to the boy who was lying just a few yards from the busy boulevard. One look was all it took for the cops and paramedics to realize that the boy was not an accident victim. He had been stabbed repeatedly in the upper chest and had what looked like defensive wounds on his legs.

Although they observed that his vital signs were weak and that he was obviously only barely alive, the attending paramedics nonetheless felt there was a "glimmer of hope" that the boy might be saved. But they couldn't save him, they knew, if they had to transport him by ground to the nearest hospital. That would take much too long and the kid, without immediate surgery, could only live a few minutes more at best. Without wasting a precious minute, they summoned the Life Flight helicopter from Emanuel Hospital, located just across the Columbia River in Portland, Oregon. They knew that Emanuel was better equipped to deal with trauma victims than were Vancouver's hospitals, but time was running out for the boy. The paramedics did what they could for the child at the scene, then transported him to Fort Vancouver High School, located just down the hill, where they waited for the helicopter to arrive. The high school was the nearest site where the helicopter could safely land. Billy was picked up by the aircraft in the school's large parking area a few minutes later.

Billy was barely breathing as a nurse and a paramedic feverishly treated his wounds during the short flight to Portland. However, despite their heroic efforts, they finally realized that there was just no way they were going to be able to save him. His injuries were too extensive, and he had lost far too much blood. He might have had a chance if they could have reached him a few minutes sooner, but they hadn't and his precious life light was fading fast. Billy, who carried no identification, was pronounced dead on arrival at the hospital at 7:37 P.M., and was listed as a "Junior Doe."

* * *

Duane Bigoni, a deputy Oregon state medical examiner, was assigned to the case because the boy had died in Oregon even though it was clear that the attack had occurred in Washington. Bigoni, who had been a pathologist for years, hated dealing with child homicide cases. Emotionally, they were always much worse to deal with than were cases that involved adult victims. When he viewed Billy's ravaged body for the first time, it was all he could do to remain composed. He simply couldn't understand how anyone could attack a child with such viciousness. It was just so cruel and inhuman.

After he examined Billy's wounds, Bigoni, shaking his head in disbelief, concurred with the investigators' opinion that the child had died of stab wounds to the chest and abdomen. But he told investigators that a definitive autopsy would still have to be done to determine the exact cause of death, just to be sure. He also pointed out that the secondary wounds on the boy's legs were defensive injuries, incurred when he tried to fight off his attacker. Although one of the police officers asked him, Bigoni could not say whether the boy had been sexually attacked. Because the child did not carry any identification in his clothes, said Bigoni, they would just have to hope that someone would miss the boy soon and report his disappearance to the police. That way they could at least get a name, often the cornerstone or building block from which a homicide investigation forged onward.

Because of their concern for the community's safety, the Vancouver Police Department promptly issued a news release about the child homicide victim. Because of the implications, namely that a child killer was on the loose, they naturally wanted to stress the importance that residents take every precaution with their children. At the same time they didn't want to unduly create a panic, so they were careful about the type of information they released.

Clair Neer was worried sick about Billy and Cole's failure to return home in time for dinner. It just wasn't like them to be so late. Neer hadn't yet heard the news about the child found at David Douglas Park. At a few minutes before 8:00 P.M., Neer decided that he could no longer just wait and hope that his boys would return home. He began a street-by-street search of the neighborhood and areas adjacent to the *east* side of David Douglas Park. He returned home an hour later after having found no trace of his boys or their bikes. Similarly, he found no one who had seen them after they left the golf course. Now more alarmed than ever, Neer called the Vancouver Police Department at 9:00 P.M. and reported Billy and Cole as missing.

When word of Neer's phone call about his missing boys filtered down to the lawmen investigating the David Douglas Park homicide, Detective Jeff Sundby, thirty-four, who had only recently been rotated into the detective squad and had caught the assignment as the lead investigator in the case, realized that there might be another body to be found. It was decided that a dozen or so searchers made up of police officers, fire fighters, and members of the Silver Star Search and Rescue team would remain at the scene where the still-unidentified boy's body had been found. They would spend the night there and continue their work as long as necessary.

Fearing that curious onlookers might interfere with their search efforts for a possible second victim, uniformed officers cordoned off the area and closed down the northbound lanes of Andresen Road later that evening.

As the park search continued, Sundby coordinated efforts to pull the investigation together and determine if their "Junior Doe" was one of the missing Neer brothers. If it turned out that he was, Sundby knew that the other Neer brother was likely dead, too, and was probably lying out there in the park somewhere. It was

Sundby's first homicide case, and he knew from the outset that if two kids turned up dead, the victims of some mad child killer, he would have a real problem on his hands. He shuddered at the mere thought of such a grim possibility.

By now fully aware of the circumstances surrounding the missing boys, Sundby and one of his superiors, Captain Bob Kanekoa, paid a visit to the Neer home. Shortly after being invited inside by Clair Neer, Kanekoa noticed a computer printout picture of two boys on a table. He immediately thought he recognized one of the boys as being the park victim, and his heart sank.

The two investigators moved carefully in their approach to Neer, who was clearly distraught with worry by that time as any parent would be if his child or children were missing. Kanekoa and Sundby didn't want to unduly alarm or distress him further by making irresponsible statements about the boy found in the park. Before they could tell him about the boy, they had to be absolutely certain that the victim was Neer's son. Along those lines, Sundby made every effort to obtain as much information about the Neer brothers as possible including physical descriptions, photographs, the clothing they were wearing when they left home, the types of bicycles they were riding, and so forth.

Meanwhile at the park, utilizing flashlights

and lanterns, one group of searchers proceeded carefully along the trails while another group beat back the bushes in their probe for evidence and, possibly, another victim. It was slow going under the conditions of night but, a short time later, the searchers found not one, but *two* children's BMX bicycles near the trail, about forty-five yards south from where Danny Miller had found Billy's body. Lieutenant Brown told a crowd of news-hungry reporters, eager to get their stories onto the 11:00 P.M. news shows and into the morning editions of the newspapers, that his investigators did not yet know for certain if one of the bikes belonged to the dead boy, but cautiously added that both bikes fit the description given to police by Clair Neer. Although he didn't reveal his feelings to the press, he now feared more than ever that the unnerving discovery meant that there might be another victim out there. As a result, Brown decided to call in extra help and expand the search.

Several hours later, at about 2:00 A.M., while searchers continued to scour the remote area for clues, a volunteer from the Silver Star Search and Rescue team found what everybody hoped they wouldn't: another victim. Unlike his brother, Cole was dead at the scene. His body was lying among heavy brush about twenty-five yards east of where the bicycles were found, right where Westley Allan Dodd had left it. Like the first victim, this boy had been stabbed in the chest and abdomen. Sundby noted that this boy, also like the first, had defensive wounds on his hands and legs, an indication that both boys had attempted to fight off their attacker before succumbing to his heartless violence.

A short time later, there was no longer any mystery to the boys' identities. Using photographs provided by Clair Neer, Sundby and Kanekoa confirmed that the victims were positively Billy and Cole Neer. Now they had the dreaded duty of informing Neer that his sons had been brutally murdered by an unknown assailant. Notifying the next of kin that a loved one had been murdered was one of the most difficult duties a police officer faced. Nearly all police officers dreaded the task, but few as much as Sundby and Kanekoa.

Billy had been found first, Sundby told the stricken father, but both had likely been attacked at about the same time. Judging by the time the boys were believed to have left the golf course and the time when Danny Miller found Billy's body, Sundby said he believed the attack had occurred between 6:15 P.M. and 6:45 P.M. He said that he had not yet uncovered a motive for the murders. When he left, Neer was sobbing and in tremendous emotional pain over

50

his loss, and Sundby found himself wondering how the grieving father would cope with it all.

"What kind of motive does someone have for killing a ten- and eleven-year-old boy?" asked Vancouver Police Captain Ray Anderson, who was at the scene with Sundby. "There are only so many possible motives in something like this. With adults, there's always the anger motive. People get mad at each other and fight. But when it's a couple of young boys cut up for no apparent reason . . . you just don't know. . . . This kind of thing just never happens in Vancouver. We can go a whole year without a homicide. These were just two brothers — spitting images of each other — out riding their bikes, and they come across an assailant. We're talking about the kinds of things that happen to other people in other places, but hopefully not to you."

According to Anderson, the boys' clothing was sent to the Washington State Crime Laboratory in Kelso, along with other evidence gathered at the crime scene, for analysis. They were hoping for a break that would lead them at least one step closer to identifying the killer. However, little of significance would be provided from the analysis, and their hope that the case could be quickly solved would be dashed. Because Cole's pants were pulled down below his knees when his body was found, the only thing that the Vancouver sleuths knew for certain was that they were looking for a sex killer who apparently had no sense of conscience. But they kept that information to themselves, for the time being.

Chapter Three

From its outset, the double murder case took on a marked intensity like none that Vancouver had ever seen before, and everyone connected with it hoped that they would never have to endure another one like it again. Nearly all cops agree that homicide cases involving children are always more intense, and strike harder than murders involving adults.

The intensity was evident throughout much of Tuesday, September 5, as Detective Jeff Sundby questioned Danny Miller, the teenager who had found mortally wounded Billy Neer and alerted the authorities, at length. Although Sundby did not publicly identify Miller as a suspect, he and his colleagues would focus on him for the next nine weeks. They would repeatedly question Miller, his family and friends, his neighbors, even his coworkers at McDonald's, ultimately to no avail. Miller simply didn't know anything about the Neer brothers' murders. His only involvement was when he found Billy's body. With good reason, Miller complained that the Vancouver detectives had gone too far in their probing of him, and maintained that he only did what any other respectable and responsible citizen would do by reporting the discovery of the injured child. How could doing the right thing result in him being placed at the top of the list of possible suspects? Miller wanted to know, in part, because his friends, neighbors, and coworkers had begun to shun him, evidently thinking that he was the killer even though the police did not have enough evidence to arrest him.

In defense of their actions, Sundby and Captain Ray Anderson said that Miller was the only person they could physically place at the crime scene. Since there was no one else, it was only natural that they would initially focus their probe on him.

"We were under extreme pressure from the public to find the child killer," said Anderson. "As a result, we probably did step on some people's toes. . . . We had to check him out and eliminate him . . . before we could go any further. It was just police procedures that were followed."

They did, of course, eventually eliminate Danny Miller as a suspect. But Miller's problems didn't end there. He ended up suffering from depression, nightmares, and paranoia, and had difficulty finding and keeping a job after the experience. He was eventually diagnosed as suffering from post-traumatic stress syndrome because of the experience, and was placed on Social Security disability benefits.

"He has too many problems, thinking people are always looking at him," said his mother. "He has his ups and downs and his sleepless nights, and he still suffers from nightmares. Every once in a while, at night, I hear him yelling and I'll come out and wake him up and talk to him."

Even while they focused on Miller as a possible suspect, the intensity of the case was also evident by the many investigators who literally combed David Douglas Park with metal detectors right after the murders in their search for evidence. At one point everyone became excited when a knife was found, but its importance as a potential clue soon diminished. The investigators were disappointed when they realized that it could not be the murder weapon. It was covered with mud and rust from having been at the location for a considerable time prior to the murders.

While a group of detectives and evidence technicians continued their work at the park, another group of uneasy and prudent police officials warned area residents to continue to take extra precautions in the David Douglas Park neighborhood of McLoughlin Heights. They advised people, especially children, not to go to the park alone, and encouraged residents to report any suspicious characters or activities in any of Vancouver's neighborhoods, particularly those in which there were parks.

Residents were also uneasy and tense in the aftermath of the child murders. Mothers and fathers could be seen in areas near David Douglas Park before school commenced and prior to dismissal on the days after the slayings. One group of neighborhood parents positioned themselves sentry-like about fifty yards apart and lined the paths that ran along the routes that many schoolchildren normally took to and from their homes. Other parents, even those who lived only a few blocks from their childrens' schools and typically allowed their kids to walk or ride their bikes to and from school, began driving their children instead.

Police and parents weren't the only ones who were jumpy in the aftermath of the Neer murders. The Vancouver School District immediately initiated a new set of standards to ensure child safety. They increased adult supervision on playgrounds and at student crossing zones, and sent letters home cautioning parents to not allow their children to take routes through secluded or wooded areas to and from school and to always walk or ride their bikes in groups. The community had clearly become unsettled, and people began to realize that every parent's worst nightmare had suddenly become a terrifying reality. Little did anyone know that Westley Allan Dodd was secretly making grisly plans for his future victims, and would soon tighten the grip of fear he now held on the community into a deadly and unrelenting stranglehold.

In an effort to better understand every aspect of the tragedy of the Neer brothers' murders, Detective Jeff Sundby and his colleagues also looked at the Neer family's background at the same time they investigated Danny Miller. Many investigators, including Sundby, subscribed to the notion that a killer can often be found somewhere in a victim's background, and they naturally had to cover all their bases if they hoped to solve the case. Although his gut feeling told him that such a notion wouldn't hold true here, Sundby couldn't dismiss the possibility without first going through the motions. Again, as with Miller, it was a process of eliminating people as suspects.

Sundby soon learned that William "Billy"

James Neer was born in Portland, Oregon, on May 8, 1979, and that Cole LaVern Neer was born in Devils Lake, North Dakota, on June 11, 1978. They also had a younger brother, Richard, who was six at the time of his brothers' murders. Although the Neers adored all three of their children and seemed genuinely happy during their first years of marriage, the family unit became marred by marital problems. A period of deep-seated unhappiness followed when it became clear that Neer and his wife, Arlene, would be unable to work out their differences. Neer and Arlene eventually divorced when the boys were still quite young. Arlene, a member of the Devils Lake Sioux Indian Tribe, decided to return to her native North Dakota and relinquished custody of the children to Neer. After the divorce was finalized, Neer moved his three boys to the Vancouver area in 1986 and first settled in the suburb of Hazel Dell. Though it was difficult at first, Neer and his boys managed to adjust to their new situation and environment in a positive manner, and for the first couple of years everything went along fairly well for the divorced father and his kids.

However, even though Neer was skilled as a glass cutter, an auto glass repairman, and a mechanic, he eventually encountered employment difficulties and was laid off from his job at a time when the economy began to turn sour and jobs were becoming scarce. When the prospect of obtaining a good job where he could utilize his skills and abilities began to seem hopeless, he and the three boys were forced by necessity to move into a public housing project in the McLoughlin Heights area of Vancouver in July, 1989. It was while living there, at 305 Council Bluffs Way, that Billy and Cole learned they could make extra money by scavenging for lost golf balls at the nearby driving range.

Neighbors told Sundby that the Neer family was quiet and kept to themselves for the most part. They were well-liked in the neighborhood, and it was common for residents to see Billy and Cole tearing down the streets of the usually quiet neighborhood on their BMX bikes on any given day.

"Those boys were always so good," said a friend and neighbor. "And they were always together, every time they went out bike riding."

"They were just babies," said the boys' aunt, who lived with them. "I can't believe anyone doing this to them."

Sundby, who could feel the family's pain and grief, could only nod his head in agreement. By now he had begun to realize that his gut feelings had been correct in that he wouldn't find the boys' killer anywhere in the family's background. Everything he learned pointed more and more toward a stranger being the killer. Though it was emotional and painful for the family to endure, Sundby knew that he had to press on and get as much information as he could. He hoped that he would be able to reconstruct Billy's and Cole's activities the day they were killed, and that the information would help him uncover clues, however minute, to their killer's identity.

Billy had been a fourth-grader and Cole a fifth-grader at Dwight D. Eisenhower Elementary School when they had lived in Hazel Dell. However, their father had recently enrolled them in Marshall Elementary School, located near their new home in McLoughlin Heights. Although they had only attended a few days of the new school year, both boys were described as sharp kids who really liked school. Records from their previous school confirmed that fact by showing that they rarely had been absent. But their real love was for each other. They regularly played baseball together, wrestled with each other, and held a mutual penchant for collecting baseball cards. They would do almost anything to make enough money to add new cards to their prized collection.

"There was a baseball card shop in the neighborhood, and the guy who owned the shop was from North Dakota, like they were, and they got along great," said Neer to reporters later. He also said that neither boy had been to the card shop the day they were killed.

"Cole, he was a real good artist for being a young kid," said Neer. "He could draw almost anything out of a book—that's why I got them an encyclopedia set. Airplanes, you name it. He had all the detail. He'd finish, and it would look perfect. If he'd had the time, he would have been really something. I'd look at the things he'd draw and see how good he was and wonder where the heck he got that (talent). Billy, he was really good at putting together model cars. He could take things apart and put them back—fix things really well. . . . They were such good little guys—they never bothered or hurt nobody."

Neer reiterated that Billy and Cole had regularly ridden their bicycles through the bike trails of David Douglas Park where they were killed, a place he had always considered safe.

"They mentioned riding their bikes through that park a lot," said Neer. "All the kids did at that park. Parks are supposed to be made for kids, right? I guess this one here isn't." He nor anyone else could offer the detectives any theories about who could have killed the boys or why.

Neer stated that he would take Billy and Cole back to North Dakota for burial. He said that he would also take his only surviving child, Richard, to Hillsboro, Oregon, where they would live with a relative.

"As soon as I step outside that door, I'm gone. I'm not going to lose my last son to this crap . . . Vancouver — I used to like it. The boys seemed to like it really well. Now, I don't want anything to do with any of it." He emphasized that he never wanted to set foot again in Vancouver, Washington, not even to drive through it.

In the face of the tragedy that had devastated his family, a mournful Clair Neer told reporters that the public needed to know what had happened to his family. It was important to him to get his message out, and it was somehow heartwrenching hearing it come from a man who had just lost most of his family to a killer without a conscience.

"For kids," he offered, "they need to know that they should listen to their parents. Something's going to happen if they don't. And they should trust nobody. And parents . . . keep an eye on your kids. Don't let them wander off too far. Losing one is bad. Losing two . . . well, all

I've got left is my baby."

Meanwhile, Sundby and his colleagues located a young boy who had been in the park late on the afternoon of the murders. He was interviewed, but said that he hadn't seen Billy and Cole. However, the boy had seen a suspicious man in the park, and apparently had gotten a good look at him. As a result, Portland police artist Jean Boylan was brought in to draw a composite sketch of the suspicious man.

The sketch, which was circulated among police officers and released to the media, depicted an eighteen- to twenty-five-year-old male with dark, curly hair that hung one-third of the way or more down his forehead. He also had a mustache. The witness indicated that he could be from five feet eight inches to five feet ten inches tall with a medium build. He was seen wearing blue jeans and a light-colored pullover shirt. But the sketch yielded little that could help the police at that time.

"This is one of those cases that is so senseless," said King, who admitted that his department needed help in solving it. He pleaded publicly for citizens who had information about other people who they might have seen in the park to come forward. "That's how these cases are made," he stressed.

A short time later another witness did, in fact, come forward, and provided the investigators with a description of a second suspicious person who was at the park at the time of the slayings. The second person was described as eighteen to thirty years old, with dark, uncombed hair. The witness told investigators that he could be five feet ten inches to six feet one inch tall, with a slender build. Unlike the first "person of interest," he did not have a mustache. He wore a light-colored pullover shirt with dark pants.

From information obtained from the witnesses, the detectives had sufficient reason to believe that both subjects frequented the park almost daily. As a result, they began showing the sketches to people in the neighborhood, who might have been in the park on Labor Day, in the offhand chance that they might run across someone who recognized one or both persons depicted in the composites. To their dismay, however, the effort produced few leads of any substance.

At one point someone suggested that the Vancouver investigators should look closely at a Clark County homicide case, investigated by the sheriff's department, in which Clair Neer had discovered the victim's body while living in the

Hazel Dell area some two years earlier. The victim had been a twenty-six-year-old man, the detectives learned, who had been stabbed to death at his residence at 8513 Northeast Caleb Road after quarrelling with his girlfriend. The girlfriend had pleaded guilty to second-degree manslaughter in connection with the death, but because the victim had been stabbed and because Clair Neer had provided information to the investigating sheriff's detectives in that case, Sundby and his colleagues naturally wanted to talk to the woman. After tracking her down, however, they quickly learned that she could not possibly have been involved in Billy's and Cole's deaths. She had an airtight alibi, and the detectives concluded that she had not held any grudges against Clair Neer for cooperating with the police in the investigation of her case. As would become the rule in their investigation, they had reached another dead end.

As one day followed another, despite two teams of three detectives working twelve-hour days, only a few additional clues trickled in to the Vancouver Police Department. It wasn't that the public was not helping; they were. In fact, more than one hundred telephone calls to investigators had been generated by the release of the composite drawings. It was just that most of the calls did not lead anywhere.

One of the telephone calls, however, had steered the detectives to a woman who claimed to have seen a man running from David Douglas Park at the approximate time the killings were believed to have occurred. The call had naturally given them hope that the woman's information might lead somewhere. But when they finished interviewing her at length, the detectives concluded that the man she had seen was one of those who had previously been reported by other witnesses. Was he the killer? Unfortunately the woman's information hadn't helped them to determine, or for that matter even to dispel, that possibility.

Other callers described vehicles that potential suspects may have been driving near the park at the time of the murders, and police were told of neighborhoods where some of these men were believed to live. Some of the callers also told the detectives where some of the potential suspects worked and, as their list continued to grow, a few of the "persons of interest" turned out to be known sex offenders. However, Sundby and his investigators ran up against a brick wall at nearly every turn. The leads just didn't pan out. Their "persons of interest" had airtight alibis, namely witnesses who could vouch for their activities and whereabouts at the time of the murders, and the known sex offenders had no recent sex crimes on their police records. Unfortunately, by mid-September the homicide probers were still at square one.

Nonetheless, Sundby and his detectives were relentless in their determination to solve the case. They backtracked again and again, and eventually found a reliable witness who told them that he had seen the Neer boys riding their bicycles from the direction of the golf course. They were riding downhill, north on Andresen Road, near the park at approximately 6:10 P.M. They also found another witness who said that he had seen the boys heading southbound, walking their bikes uphill along Andresen within the same time frame. When all was said and done, however, the detectives had only been able to retrace the boys' activities up to about 6:10 P.M. They were left without clues about their movements from that time until the time Billy's body was discovered by Danny Miller at 6:50 P.M.

At the request of the Vancouver Police Department, the FBI in Washington, D.C., worked up a psychological profile of the possible killer. The profile suggested that the killer likely lived in the community, and probably was very familiar with the area and David Douglas Park. The profile also suggested that the killer could have known the two boys, and that he was likely physically large enough to easily overpower them. But because the victims were kids, he didn't necessarily have to be an exceptionally large person to overpower them to gain the "control" that he so craved. Due to the nature of the deaths, it was clear that the killer was comfortable with knives and may have used a knife in a previous assault or killing. Because of the senselessness of the crime, the profile suggested that the killer could have been "acting out in response to a significant traumatic experience that happened to him in a close time frame" with the murders.

The profile was a typical one, largely general in its approach due to the fact that so little was known about the killer at this point due to the scarcity of clues. Although Vancouver investigators appreciated the FBI's efforts in providing them with the psychological profile, many expressed frustration that it hadn't brought them any closer to collaring a suspect. All it had done, in reality, was to provide them with a trickle of insight into the mind of the type of killer with whom they were likely dealing. They conceded that it might be useful to them at some point, but it wasn't of much help to them now.

Toward the end of September, when the case seemed destined for failure, the detectives ferreted out yet another witness who provided them with a new lead. A passing motorist informed the investigators that he had seen two young boys, whom he believed to have been the Neer brothers, in the vicinity of the park at about 6:30 P.M. on Labor Day. The boys had been only a few yards from one of the park's trail heads, talking to a man.

"Both of them had their bikes, and they were standing in the middle of the road, on the median strip, talking to this individual," said Captain Ray Anderson, relating the witness's statement. The man in question was in his late teens to early twenties and had dark hair. He was on foot. Unfortunately, the witness was unable to provide other details such as a description of the clothing the man was wearing.

"It leads us to the possibility that, whoever this person was, he could well be the assailant." The new witness, at the very least, had moved the time line of the boys' movements closer to when Billy was found by Danny Miller, and his statement had given the detectives hope that the witness had seen the assailant. If he had, he might be able to identify him from a police lineup later, when a suspect was apprehended. But, everyone realized, it was just as possible that the person seen talking to the Neer brothers had not been the killer. He may have been only an innocent passerby, much like Danny Miller had been.

To everyone's disillusionment, no new leads surfaced, and the unknown man seen talking to Billy and Cole Neer remained a mystery.

Chapter Four

While the detectives from the Vancouver Police Department ran down one fruitless lead after another in an investigation that took its toll on them mentally and physically, Westley Allan Dodd spent his evenings after work sitting alone in his small duplex apartment planning his next hunt. Soon after he murdered the Neer brothers, he wrote in his diary that he had decided the next time he "must spend more time with the boy (or girl?) before killing," and would make sure that "the body is hidden better."

He began to study area maps and conscientiously marked off locations both in Vancouver and in Portland, across the Columbia River in Oregon, where he felt he would have the greatest success finding children to molest and murder. Most of the locations he marked off were parks and school playgrounds, and he kept telling himself that he would soon begin visiting them to check them out, much as a thief would "case" the place he intended to burglarize, as he had done at David Douglas Park.

He also spent a lot of time reading the newspapers, as much to relive the Neer murders in fantasies as to find out just how much the cops really knew about the killer. When he was finished reading, he always clipped out the newspaper articles and attached them to his notebook. Afterward he would take out his diary of death from his briefcase, which he kept locked and hidden safely beneath his bed, and make his entries on any given day. The following entry from Wednesday, September 6, 1989, a mere two days after the Neer murders, serves as an example:

While most of my future victims will die (in various ways), I also hope to have some long relationships with children as well. . . . I'd like to make some child porno movies. I also hope to get "before and after" photos of my "sex-murder" victims as well.

When crotch fucking the ones to die, I'll clean the kid real well before killing, and deposit my sperm in something to remove it as "forensic evidence." When butt fucking, I'll use a well-greased rubber (may fuck either way before *or after* they die, depending on whether they're bloody or not). Some of them will also be forced to perform certain acts on me.

I think I got more of a high out of killing than molesting. I had fantasized previously of my stomach against a boy's back, my arms around him, and over his arms. He is blindfolded so as not to see the knife I'm holding to a point just below his breast bone. . . .

Just read—you'll see what actually does occur. Just writing this and (reading) previous story about my first murder makes my cock stiff. I must find it sexual. I'll note that *The Oregonian* is a morning paper and *The Columbian* an afternoon paper.

The news articles will be numbered in the order they appeared. The same number on different articles indicate they all came from same edition of paper. #1 is two different articles, being about the killing, then about the boys' lives. Police don't even know Cole was molested—even though his pants were down! Maybe that's the way to go—leave no indication of a rape?—NAW—too much I want to do would be obvious.

Often when Dodd finished writing a diary entry, he masturbated himself to climax while he fantasized about murdering Billy and Cole Neer, or some other child that he had sexually molested or exposed himself to, and then would go to bed. His sociopathic mind rarely allowed him to worry about anything that he had done to others, and when he did fret about something he'd done it was purely out of concern for self-preservation and not out of remorse for his victims.

It wasn't until Thursday, September 7, that any of the news reports about the Neer murders gave him cause to worry. Up until that point the news reports had induced only mild concern. But the article that had appeared in *The Columbian,* Vancouver's daily, that day had very much alarmed him. It described how the police had talked to kids and other witnesses who had been at the park on the day of the killings, and how a police artist had drawn a sketch of a man seen at the park that day. The sketch, Dodd realized as he looked at it in horror, actually *resembled* him. While it didn't come close to being an exact likeness of him, certain features, particularly the eyes and the mustache, were strikingly accurate. He quickly decided that he would have to spend more time at home, indoors, for a while, and would go out only when necessary to avoid being recognized. He also considered changing his appearance in some way, such as wearing a hat.

That same evening, shortly before dark, Dodd had another unpleasant experience that gave him even more cause for alarm than had the composite sketch in the newspaper. He suddenly heard several cars pull up in front of the house where he was renting a room, and without hesitation he jumped up from his writing table and ran to the window. When he looked out he saw, much to his horror, three cruisers from the Clark County Sheriff's Department. With his heart in his throat, he stood back and watched as several deputies approached the entrance to his landlady's portion of the house. He paced back and forth while they were inside talking to her, and frequently looked out of the window to see if they were coming over to his apartment. The time that passed seemed like hours to him, and he desperately wanted to know what was happening. Finally, a few minutes later he heard the deputies emerge from his landlady's apartment. To his relief they got in their cars and left.

But what had they wanted? He continued to wonder as he paced nervously around his room. Had they been there asking questions about the murders? David Douglas Park was, after all, less than a mile away. Had someone reported seeing him, the person in the sketch, in the neighborhood? He wanted desperately to go over and ask his landlady, Berniece Walker*, sixty-eight, what the deputies had wanted. But did he dare? Unable to withstand the suspense any longer, Dodd decided that he had to go over and talk to Berniece. She would either put his mind to rest, or he would have to make fast tracks out of there.

Afterward, he was glad that he had gone to her apartment. Berniece had told him that the sheriff's deputies came because she had called them following a verbal argument with another tenant that she had evicted earlier. Dodd eventually turned the conversation to the murders in David Douglas Park, and asked her if it was possible that the guy she had evicted was the killer. She told him that she didn't think so. The person they were looking for was "shorter and darker" than the man that she had evicted. Dodd continued talking about the murders, and told Berniece that he hoped the police would catch the killer soon. When he returned to his room he realized, to his relief, that the sheriff's deputies hadn't been interested in him at all. He was short, but certainly not dark.

For the next several days, Dodd continued to follow the news reports about the police manhunt for the Neer brothers' killer. He hoped to find out if the police had found "anything on the boys' crotches," such as semen, but nothing in the news articles had even hinted about the forensic evidence. He had been careful not to leave any semen or other evidence on the boys that could link him to the crime, so he was fairly confident, but not certain, that none had been found. All he learned from the news articles was that there was no obvious evidence that either boy had been sexually assaulted. Dodd finally realized that the police had deliberately withheld from the media the fact that Cole's pants were pulled down below his knees when his body was discovered.

The 11:00 P.M. news on Tuesday, September 12, revealed that two new sketches of "persons of interest" had been released by the police, and were shown on television. As the composites flashed across his television screen, Dodd saw that neither sketch resembled him at all. He suddenly realized that there was nothing for him to worry about. The police were not on to him, and it didn't appear likely that they would be, at least not in the foreseeable future. Nonetheless, he decided that he would stay away from David Douglas Park for a while, just in case a kid who had been there on Labor Day might see him and remember that he had been there on Labor Day, too.

As one day followed another, Dodd continued to fantasize and make his plans for future kills. Unable to go out and hunt for children at his usual haunts of parks and movie theaters out of fear of being recognized from the first composite that had made the news, Dodd resigned himself to continue to lay low for the time being. As a substitute for going out, he began to graphically enter many of his most gruesome thoughts into his diary:

. . . Just had a brilliant thought. I must purchase an *audio* cassette recorder. That way I'll later be able to log exact words and reaction descriptions during a rape, molest, operation, murder, etc. That will do until I can afford the more expensive camcorder with sound. Kidnap victims will not be told anything until I can do it on tape. . . .

. . . In surgery with live patients, whether they are conscious or not, they'll have to be tied down. Hands loosely over head to keep them from coming into the way. To prevent bouncing, tied tightly to table around chest and waist, possibly abdomen also. Tie at knees to maintain legs at desired location, and at ankles to keep feet down. May do surgery with or without pain relief or sedation.

At the end of the preceding passage Dodd, very much sexually aroused, drafted a crudely drawn "torture rack" which he intended to build out of wood. It was something that he had been thinking about building for a long time, but had just never gotten around to doing. He was always busy working or trolling for kids to molest. Now, perhaps, since he had to keep a low profile for a while, he might have the time to actually build it. When he was finished, the drawing chillingly depicted a securely bound child lying on the rack. Directly below it, he penciled in the words "live kids" and set them off in parentheses. When he finished with the "blueprint," he continued with the entries to his diary, some of which included details about the methods of killing he would use on his victims:

Can obtain unconsciousness by keeping them awake late, then giving several sleeping pills.

Murder Methods:

Fastest: Stabbing
           Slicing Throat. Too Messy!!!
Slowest: Starvation/Thirst
   Slow: Bleeding to death (blood could
           be caught in jars)
Medium: Suffocation
           Drowning

Uses/possibilities

(1) Drown; (2) hang by neck; (3) plastic bag over face; (4) strangle (with hands or rope); (5) pillow tight over face; (6) hog-tie and tape over nose and mouth; (7) amputate privates a little at a time until bled dead; (8) stab; (9) slice throat (too messy!); (10) no food and/or water; (11) drugs (full bottle sleeping pills?); (12) start experimental surgery on live, conscious, blindfolded, tied-down victims.

. . . For my first incident, knife was best choice as my kill would have to be quick and easy for the chosen location. Decided that this (next) incident would have a cleaner kill—probably choking, to have a clean body. . . . I want a better location for this incident, so I feel more comfortable and can take more time for various types of sex before [and after] killing the child.

One possibility is kidnapping — at home I'd have all the time I need. One thing for certain is for this incident the sex will take longer, and death will be something different than stabbing. . . .

In the following excerpt from Dodd's diary, he explained how he had made a pact with Satan, something that he later said he wasn't serious about. As the passage progresses, Dodd's immaturity again shows through and he seems almost childlike himself in making his "request":

. . . I bought a set of X-acto knives and tweezers last night, giving me the necessary tools for my "exploratory surgeries." I've now asked Satan to provide me with "a 6-10 year old boy to make love to, suck and fuck, play with, photograph, kill, and do my exploratory surgery on." On my legs and groin, I wrote, "I now have needed tools for surgery." And I took a nude nap from 4:00-5:30, and dozed until about 6:30 this afternoon.

I now ask Satan that this boy be an easy target; meaning, due to heat from Incident

#1, I can't do much "hunting" for fear of being "noticed" by a "witness."

If the conditions on the previous page are met, and I can remain sexually satisfied, through contact, pictures, or tapes, then I will gladly turn my soul over to Satan.

Dodd continued to slip in and out of these fantasy states throughout September, as his diary entries indicate, and at one point he began to make plans to kidnap and secretly keep a child, for the sole purpose of sex. He decided that when one child became too old, he would simply dispose of him and find a "fresh one." He even went so far in his thoughts to decide that he would lock up or tie and gag his captive while he was at work or out shopping.

He continued to study maps of the Vancouver/Portland area, and finally chose several primary "possible kidnap sites" as well as "secondary locations to take the child to for the kill." He even considered driving to far away locations such as Yakima and the Tri-Cities (Richland, Kennewick, and Pasco) in the eastern part of the state where he grew up, but decided that he would have to wait until his financial situation improved enough to allow him to make the longer trips.

By Sunday, September 24, Dodd's growing frustration stemming from his need to find a new victim apparently had driven him further into a fantasy state. He began to dwell on "experimental surgeries" again, and that evening drew a neatly sketched diagram of the male reproductive system after studying the set of encyclopedias he kept in a small bookcase next to his bed. The diagram was very detailed and included such anatomical features as the bladder, seminal vesicle, prostate gland, urethra, vas deferens, penis, epididymis, and testicles. When he was finished, he sat back and admired his handiwork, as was his custom. Apparently he was so impressed that he felt compelled or driven to expound on his grisly plans in an essay of sorts that he appropriately titled, *For Dead Experiments,* which included detailed descriptions of the "experimental surgery" he would perform and other plans such as:

Would like to videotape the exploratory, as well as future "operations," to use as future reference, to show "patients" what I'll be doing, or to "terrify" victims, if I wish to do so, but at this time (9-24-89/8:15 p.m.), I don't think I want to merely "terrify" them.

83

10:30 p.m. In surgery on live "patients," with or without "patient's" consent, they'll be tied down. . . .

I could induce unconsciousness by keeping them up late, then giving them several sleeping pills, which would allow me to do things that may otherwise be painful for them. . . .

. . . 11:15 p.m. Thoughts of getting (a child or two) for a period of time . . . (that could) be taught Lucifer's ways, and be an assistant to Lucifer, through me, until they're able to work on their own, or get too old and are used as a possible sacrifice. . . .

11:45 p.m. The last couple of days I've really been wanting a child. I hope something happens soon.

Nothing, however, aside from nurturing his grossly violent fantasies, happened for Dodd during the remaining days of September. But something *would* happen soon, before the month of October came to an end. It would be something so horrible, so horrendous and vile, that it would leave the residents of the Pacific Northwest reeling with disgust for years to come.

Chapter Five

Despite all of his careful planning and wishful thinking, Westley Allan Dodd somehow managed to make it through most of the month of October without molesting or killing any children. By his own admission, as evidenced by the entries in his diary, he had waited patiently for things to cool down regarding the murders of Billy and Cole Neer before resuming the hunt for his next victim. Regardless of what other serial killers had said to the contrary after they had been caught, Dodd was one serial killer who didn't *want* to get caught. He liked what he was doing so much that he couldn't even begin to entertain the possibility of spending his life imprisoned in a ten-square-foot cell the size of a parking space. That was why he was nearly always reluctant to take uncalled for chances, and tried, whenever possible, to exercise restraint by giving in to his unnatural urges only when he was certain that the outcome would be successful. He had also been working a great deal at that time, and that had played a part, at least temporarily, in helping to keep him from getting too excited about kids.

By Friday evening, October 27, however, his libido had begun to bring out the worst in him again. He didn't fully understand what brought on his evil impulses, but he somehow knew and accepted it. When Dodd felt that the urge to molest and kill was creeping back into his conscious mind, he began making plans on how to best spend his weekend. While sitting at his writing table that evening, Dodd decided that the perfect time to "find" his next boy would be on his way home from work the next day, a Saturday, between 3:30 P.M. and 4:00 P.M. That way he'd be able to keep the kid alive from 4:00 P.M. Saturday to 4:00 P.M. Sunday, his day off, at which time he could kill the child for his "experiments" and be able to get rid of the corpse before going back to work on Monday.

As he wandered in and out of a fantasy state, Dodd found himself wanting to have sex with his next victim "a time or two, or more if time allows, then kill for dead sex, photos, experiments, and the exploratory—using what I learn to later operate on live boys. Perfect would be a 3-year-old to kill and a 6- to 8-year-old to help with surgery. I'd later hang the nude 6- to 8-year-old and photograph him dying. Just writing this makes me quite erect. . . ." Prior to turning in for the night, Dodd masturbated himself to climax to release some of the sexual tension that had been building up over the previous several hours.

Dodd went to work the next day as planned, but was disappointed and became agitated when he wasn't able to find a boy on his way home. After considering the places where the most kids might go on a weekend night, he finally decided that he would check out Oaks Park in Portland after dinner. And if he had no luck there, he would go to a movie. If that, too, failed to produce a suitable boy for him, he decided that he would try another park in Portland on Sunday where he hoped that the "hunting (would) be as it was at David Douglas Park in Incident #1."

It was about 5:30 P.M. when Dodd arrived at Oaks Park, an amusement center situated near the east bank of the Willamette River beneath Portland's Sellwood Bridge. The park was much like a carnival with rides for children and adults, food and game booths, even a large roller skating rink. It was nearly always crowded, especially on Saturday nights, which Dodd knew would make it easier for him to separate children from their parents or from older siblings and babysitters. It was Dodd's first visit to the park, and he was enthralled. Kids were everywhere, and it was noisy. He blended right in with the crowds, and no one paid him any mind as he began to single out possible choices.

He soon saw one boy, about eight years old,

standing near a ride called "The Spider." Dodd strolled over to him, thumbs in the waistband of his jeans, and began making idle conversation. He told the boy that he had something he wanted to show him, and was nearly able to convince the child to follow him to a secluded area at one end of the park. But just as they were about to leave, an adult got off one of the rides and started walking toward them. Dodd, as soon as he realized that the adult was with the kid, took that as his cue to get out of there. He had blown it, and he knew that the kid would probably tell the adult about the man who had tried to get him to go with him. Dodd left Oaks Park half an hour after he arrived, more frustrated than ever.

On his way back home, Dodd drove through the streets of Southeast Portland, looking for a new hunting ground. At about 6:20 P.M. he saw movement around the poorly lit Richmond School located at Southeast Forty-first Street and Grant Avenue. He liked what he saw—the lights at the school weren't even on. The movement he had seen in the dark turned out to be teens and adults who were, of course, of no interest to him. But when he circled the school again, he saw three small kids who looked to be about seven to nine years old. To Dodd, younger and weaker victims were always best.

He circled again, intending to stop and approach them after deciding that he would tell one of the kids that he would have to come with him. He would send the other two kids in the opposite direction so that they wouldn't be able to see his car. He figured it was so dark that they couldn't get a good enough look at him to provide an accurate description to the cops later. But after circling the block he discovered, much to his dismay, that they had disappeared. He spent another fifteen minutes searching for them, but found no trace of the boys. He reluctantly returned to Vancouver, his demented desires again having gone unfulfilled.

Unwilling to call it a night, Dodd drove to a theater located inside Vancouver Mall where a children's movie called *The Bear* was showing. He arrived at 7:30 P.M. and took a seat at the rear of the auditorium, where he could easily watch the kids who left to go to the snack bar or to the bathroom.

After watching a good deal of the movie, as well as several children who came and went, Dodd finally settled on a boy about five years old. Dodd waited a minute or so after the boy left the auditorium before getting out of his seat, afraid that he would arouse someone's suspicion if he jumped right up and left at the same moment that the boy passed by him. He went toward the bathroom, intending to say, "Come with me," after which he would take the boy out of the theater and to his apartment. But the boy came out of the bathroom just as Dodd was about to go in. He had waited too long before going after the kid.

Frustrated over having had his plans foiled again, Dodd told himself via his diary that he should have known that a kid would not take much time going to the bathroom. A child would want to get back to the movie as soon as possible. Angry at himself for having failed so miserably, Dodd vowed that he would try again the next day. He would attempt to find a boy at a park, or perhaps return to Richmond School's playground. If he failed to get what he wanted there, he would just have to go to two or three movies in the afternoon to find his next victim.

The next day, Sunday, October 29, Dodd left home at 10:30 A.M. to buy film for a Polaroid camera he had purchased a few days earlier. After loading the film into the camera, he headed toward Portland and arrived at the Richmond School playground at 11:30 A.M. After he parked his car, he saw two eight- to nine-year-old boys and a four- to five-year-old boy a short distance away from the older kids. He watched them for a few minutes and, unable to determine if they were all together, decided not to risk an abduction just yet.

Dodd drove to a nearby park he had seen the day before, but there weren't any children there. He waited for about twenty minutes, and when none showed up he drove back to Richmond School. The boys were still there, he observed as he circled the block. He saw another three- to four-year-old boy, whom he thought was with an adult. But when he parked his car, a yellow 1974 Ford Pinto station wagon, on Sherman Street, on the opposite side of the school from where the kids were playing, he realized that the adult he thought he saw was only about twelve years old.

Dodd leaned up against a telephone pole and watched the kids in the playground for a while. One bigger kid and his little brother left, and two eight- to nine-year-old boys were playing with a football toward the far end of the school. Another eight- to nine-year-old boy sat on a playground structure and watched the other boys as they passed the ball back and forth to each other, their backs to Dodd and yet another boy, four to five years old, who was playing by himself on a mound known as "the volcano." The mound was a solid climbing structure made out of concrete, at the top of which there was a slide that led down the other side. The boy, who was approximately twenty feet to Dodd's left, seemed to be having a lot of fun as he climbed the stairs to the top and slid down the other side. After growing tired of the slide, the little boy moved over to the base of the mound and played quietly by himself.

After watching him for a few more minutes, Dodd walked over to the little boy. When Dodd said, "Hi," the little blond-haired boy looked up at him and smiled. God, he was beautiful, Dodd thought. He was perfect for what he wanted. Dodd, brimming with confidence, smiled back.

"Would you like to have some fun and make some money?" Dodd asked the boy. The boy seemed unsure at first, but was not frightened by Dodd. Finally, he shook his head no.

"Come on," Dodd urged, still smiling. "This will be fun." Dodd reached out his hand, and the boy took it. They walked together toward the end of the school building, and soon walked out of sight of the other kids—unseen by anyone.

"We're going to get in my car," Dodd told the child as they walked hand-in-hand.

"I don't want any money," said the child, probably remembering what his dad always told him about never getting inside a car with a stranger. Dodd picked him up and held him in front of him.

"We're still going," Dodd told him, smiling. "Let's go ask your dad if you can go with me." The mere mention of going to see his dad seemed to allay what little fear, if any, that the boy had about going with Dodd. When they got to Dodd's car, he put the child inside through the driver's side, and within seconds they were driving away from the school.

"I live the other way," protested the child when he realized that the man wasn't taking him home to talk to his dad after all.

"We're going to my house and play some games," explained Dodd. "Just do what I tell you and I promise I won't hurt you. But you'll have to be quiet when we get there. My landlady doesn't like little kids."

When they were a few blocks from the school, Dodd asked the boy his name. The child dauntlessly told the killer that his name was Lee and, holding up four fingers, he told Dodd that he was four years old. Worried that his brother would miss him while he was gone, Lee started to cry a couple of times during the short trip to Vancouver. But Dodd reached out and held his hand again, and assured him that he would be okay and that they would have some fun, just like his brother was having fun with his friends.

It was 1:30 P.M. when they arrived at Dodd's apartment. Both the landlady and the other tenant were gone, Dodd observed. It was perfect, almost too good to be true. Dodd picked up Lee and started to carry him from the car, but the boy protested.

"I can walk," said Lee. He put Lee down; and Lee, in his inviolate innocence, followed Westley Allan Dodd into his apartment.

Chapter Six

It was about 1:30 P.M. on October 29 when Robert L. Iseli, thirty-five, called 911 to report that his four-year-old son, Lee Joseph Iseli, was missing. He told the dispatcher .that Lee had failed to return home after playing at the Richmond School playground with his older brother, Justin, nine. Furthermore, his subsequent search of the neighborhood had failed to turn up any sign of the boy. Within minutes of receiving the call, Officer W.F. Brown from the Portland Police Bureau's East Precinct arrived at the Iseli home, located in the 3200 block of Southeast Clinton Street. Iseli, obviously concerned that his son had become lost or had fallen victim to foul play, met Brown at the door and invited him inside.

Iseli explained that at approximately 11 A.M. Lee, Justin, and a neighbor boy named Mark Prestwood* left the house after saying that they were going to walk up to the playground at Richmond School, located nine blocks away. Justin was enrolled in the fourth grade there, said Iseli, so he was familiar with the area. The boys enjoyed going to the playground and went there often after school and on weekends. The last time they had been there together was late on Thursday afternoon. Iseli said that he always made it a point to tell his boys and their friends to stay together, to look out for each other, and to be especially wary of strangers even though they had never had any problems in the past. However, sometime between 1:00 P.M. and 1:30 P.M. that Sunday, Justin had returned home without Lee and was crying.

According to what Justin had told his father, Lee was playing on "the volcano" the last time that he had seen him, which had been at approximately 1:00 P.M. Minutes earlier Justin, while playing on other playground equipment, looked up and observed that Lee was talking to a man, but he had been unable to hear the conversation. He ran over and told Lee not to talk to strangers, and cautioned him to yell out for him if the man did anything unusual. When he next looked toward "the volcano" a few minutes later, he noticed that Lee was gone, and so was the man. Unable to find Lee, Justin rushed home and told his father of the disappearance.

Justin described the man who had been talking to his brother as a white male, thirty-two to thirty-eight years old, approximately five feet ten

95

inches tall with a thin build. He had short brown hair and a mustache that did not extend below his upper lip, and about two to three days growth of beard stubble. He was wearing a blue baseball cap with red lettering on the front, blue jeans, and a blue T-shirt.

Iseli told Officer Brown that Lee had never walked home alone from the school before, but might know the way. He gave Brown a recent photo of Lee, and provided the officer a physical description of his son. Lee was three feet eight inches tall, weighed thirty to thirty-five pounds, and had blond hair that grew over his ears with bangs in the front. When Lee left home that morning, he was wearing a gray zipper-type warm-up jacket with a one-inch red stripe that ran down the length of each sleeve, a white T-shirt with the inscription "1989" and the words "We smoked it, Ranch Roast" on the front, khaki- or tan-colored trousers, and brown leather shoes.

"He's not a bad kid, but he does get into trouble sometimes," said Iseli, who Brown could tell was becoming more visibly upset with each passing minute. "Lee's the kind of kid who doesn't take off, but he can get sidetracked easily."

Brown wrote up the report, which became Case Number 89-100170, and had it sent out over the teletype to all police agencies in the area. Brown assured Robert Iseli that he and the department would do everything they could to find Lee.

"Four year olds don't run away," said Detective David W. Simpson, a spokesman for the Portland Police Bureau, upon learning about the missing child. "We're getting very concerned, especially as time goes on." Simpson said that if Lee had simply become lost, someone would have likely reported finding him within a relatively short period of time.

Because of Lee's age and the fact that a suspicious man had been present where he was playing, the Portland Police Bureau immediately began search efforts throughout the boy's Southeast Portland neighborhood. To expedite matters, two experienced dog handlers promptly brought in three bloodhounds in an attempt to track Lee's scent.

There was no question that the dogs picked up Lee's scent on the school playground, but they quickly lost it at the curb on Southeast Forty-first Avenue and Sherman Street. When they turned around and went the other direction, the dogs tracked Lee's scent to the area of a Kienow's grocery store at Southeast Thirty-ninth Avenue and Division Street, approximately two blocks away. Again, the dogs abruptly stopped tracking at the store. The police officers and the dog handlers didn't like the way things looked. The fact that the dogs stopped tracking at those locations indicated that Lee may have been picked up by someone in a car at either the store or at the curb by the school playground.

When officers made inquiries to the clerks of the Kienow's grocery store, they were told that Lee had in fact been inside the store after 1:00 P.M., wandering the aisles alone and looking at candy. Store employees insisted that they were certain of the time that they had seen the boy because it had been right after the beginning of the 1:00 P.M. lunch break.

"I figure if he would have left with that guy (at the school)," Robert Iseli told the probers, "why would they go to the store? Lee wasn't seen with anybody at the store. If the guy stayed outside and gave him some money to go in and buy something, Lee wasn't the kind of kid who would have just wandered around. He would have spent the money. He's never wandered off before. It's really hard to say what happened, whether he's just wandering around someplace or what. It might be that he saw some kids and went off and played with them.

He could have wandered into somebody's garage or basement.

"It may be that he's just around, that he thinks he's in trouble and is afraid to come out," added Iseli, a hopeful tone in his voice.

But as the day wore on, no further trace of Lee Iseli was found. Lee's family, as well as the police, began to fear the worst had happened. Due to the seriousness of the situation, more than a dozen police officers and volunteers fanned out in the neighborhood in a coordinated grid search that encompassed an area that extended east from Southeast Twenty-eighth Avenue to Southeast Forty-fourth Street and south from Southeast Harrison Street to Southeast Taggart Street. The grid search involved making visual examinations of residence exteriors as well as door-to-door contact with residents. Fliers bearing Lee's photograph and description were also prepared and distributed throughout the area and to members of the local media. Sergeant Brad Ritschard of East Precinct also notified the Tri-Met bus system and the local cab companies about the missing boy. In short, it was an all-out effort to find Lee Iseli, one of the most intense search efforts ever conducted by the Portland Police Bureau for a missing person. However, through no fault of the Bureau, it was doomed from the beginning to end in failure.

As near-frantic family members waited by the telephone for any information about Lee's whereabouts, many people became concerned about the possibility of the boy having to spend the night outdoors. They were afraid that he might suffer from exposure because of the near-freezing temperature. Nobody knew that he was being kept inside Wes Dodd's Vancouver apartment.

Shortly after 9:00 P.M. and still no sign of Lee, Sergeant Ritschard put in an official request for detective assistance. As a result, missing persons detectives M.D. Tellinghusen and C.J. Lovenborg were instructed to report to the Iseli residence. When they arrived, they were informed of the exhaustive search that had been conducted earlier, and they read the reports of all the officers who had taken part. Nonetheless, they found themselves going over a lot of ground that had already been covered, to no avail.

At one point Tellinghusen and Lovenborg learned of a four-year-old boy with whom Lee frequently played. They obtained the boy's name and address, and although they figured that it was a long shot they paid a late evening visit to the child's home. The boy was already in bed, they were told, but his parents said they could probably answer most of the detectives' questions.

"Lee went all over the neighborhood on foot while following his brother, Justin, who often rode his bike in the area," said Lee's friend's mother. It was typical, the police knew, for parents to let their kids roam around and play in that neighborhood, as well as most other Portland neighborhoods, with little or no supervision. Nobody had ever had a reason to keep their kids inside under lock and key, until now. "Lee and our son generally played close by when they were together," the detectives were told, but the children were prone to wander off from time to time.

"Are there any particular places that Lee and your son liked to play?" asked Lovenborg. "Are there any places that they liked to run off to and hide?"

"As a matter of fact there is," answered the mother. "There's a house on the corner of Southeast Thirty-second Avenue and Division where the boys could hide. It's a vacant house."

Lovenborg passed the information on to Sergeant Ritschard, who promptly checked the house. It was dark when he got there and, just like he had expected, he found no sign of Lee when he went inside.

By the end of the day the only known acquaintance of Lee Iseli's that police had been unable to locate was the boy's mother, Jewel Cornell, thirty-four. Tellinghusen and Lovenborg learned that Lee was in the custody of his father, and Cornell had not had any contact with Lee for quite some time. The detectives began to wonder if maybe they were dealing with a case of custodial interference, perhaps a parental abduction. Such things weren't unheard of, and this case seemed to have the right ingredients: separated parents, one with custody, and a missing child.

When they went to Cornell's last known address, a few blocks from the Iseli residence, the investigators learned that she had recently moved. After being informed that she worked at a nearby Safeway grocery store on Thirty-ninth Avenue and Powell Boulevard, they drove there with the hope of locating her. However, adding to their mounting frustration, they learned that she was not working that day and was not scheduled to work until the following evening.

Meanwhile, Tellinghusen and Lovenborg were told that Cornell was staying at a motel located in the Hollywood District of Portland. The two investigators drove to that area of town on the city's northeast side and checked with the front desk clerks at the four largest motels. However, a review of the guest lists at the Mid-Town Motel, the Hollywood Budget Inn, the Jade Tree Inn, and the Dunes Motel proved negative. If Cornell was staying at one of the motels, they reasoned, she wasn't listed in the guest registers. Since little else could be done that evening, unless new developments occurred, two East Precinct officers were assigned to assist throughout the night at the Iseli residence just in case they were needed.

The next day suspicions that a custodial abduction had occurred were quickly allayed when Jewel Cornell, along with a friend, were located at a motel on Southeast Eighty-second Avenue. When it was clear that Cornell did not have Lee with her and had not seen him for a long time, police officers informed her of her son's mysterious disappearance. She took the news hard, and although she wanted to help in the search for her boy she knew there was little that she could do. She just didn't know anything that could assist the police. The outlook became more bleak with each passing hour.

The next evening, Monday, October 30, Sergeant Larry Neville requested that homicide Detective Charles "C. W." Jensen, thirty-four, step in and continue the investigation of the missing boy. Even though there was nothing that indicated Lee Iseli was dead, it was the Portland Police Bureau's policy to put a homicide detective on the most suspicious of the missing persons cases, particularly when all other avenues had been exhausted. It was 6:00 P.M. when Jensen officially entered the case, and he began by contacting Robert Iseli and Justin at their home. By that time, it seemed highly unlikely to everyone concerned that Lee had simply become disoriented and was unable to find his way home.

Robert Iseli explained to Jensen that he had been separated from Lee's mother since February, 1986, and had lived with his mother and his two sons since that time. Iseli and Jewel Cornell were still legally married, he said, despite the continuing separation. Since their separation, Cornell had virtually no contact with Iseli or their sons. He said that he maintained a good relationship with Cornell's parents, the boys' maternal grandparents whom Justin and Lee visited approximately three or four times a year on holidays. He told Jensen that because of the good relationship among the relatives there could be no reason for any family member to abduct Lee.

Jensen next spoke with Justin, who appeared healthy and well-dressed. They sat across from each other at a table in the kitchen. Justin appeared nervous to the detective, as any kid might under similar circumstances, and had difficulty maintaining eye contact with Jensen.

"So tell me, Justin, exactly what happened yesterday," said Jensen. "I know you've already told other policemen, but I want to hear it from you. Start at the beginning."

Justin explained in a nervous and subdued voice that he and Lee had awakened on Sunday at 6:00 A.M. They didn't leave home, however, until approximately 11:00 A.M. with their neighbor Mark to go to Richmond School to play. They walked down the south side of Division Street, and stopped briefly at a video store at Thirty-fifth Avenue to look at the new Nintendo games through the window since the store was closed. When they left the video store, they continued to Thirty-ninth Avenue, where they crossed the busy street in the crosswalk, and walked to the Kienow's store on the opposite corner. That could explain, thought Jensen, why the bloodhounds had picked up Lee's scent at the store.

Justin said that Mark went inside the Kienow's store for a few minutes while he and Lee waited outside by the front doors. When Mark came out of the store, they walked on over to the school.

When they arrived at the school playground, Justin said that he saw Ricky Stevens* and Mike Dobson*, two other boys about his age, and ran over and began playing football with them. Lee went over to the volcano structure where he played by himself for some time. At one point, however, Lee came over to where Justin was playing ball and bumped into him, hard enough to make Lee cry. While trying to calm him down, Justin noticed that Lee's shoes were untied. He said he told Lee to sit down on a nearby bench where he tied his shoes for him. After Justin tied his brother's shoes, Lee sat on the bench for a few minutes more and then ran back and began playing on the volcano again.

A short time later Justin looked toward the volcano and saw Lee talking to a man. He described the man for Jensen, just as he had done for Officer Brown and his dad. Justin said that the man was standing partially on the structure, only a few feet from Lee. Justin repeated his story about how, when he saw Lee talking to the man, he had run up to the volcano and told Lee not to talk to strangers. As soon as Lee said, "Okay," Justin climbed up the volcano, went down the slide, and ran back to play with his friends. As he was running away, he said he noticed that the man was still standing near Lee.

"Why did you let your brother stay there, near the man?" asked Jensen.

"I don't know," replied Justin. "I just ran over to the fort." The fort, he told Jensen, was another playground structure about twenty feet from the volcano. He explained that it was while he was playing on the fort that he looked toward the volcano and noticed that his brother was missing.

Jensen and Justin drove to the playground so that Jensen could familiarize himself with the location and the surrounding area. He had Justin show him where he was playing when Lee disappeared. Justin led him to the structure the kids called the fort, and Jensen noted that it was approximately fifteen to twenty feet from the volcano which was in clear view of the fort structure. If Lee had called out for help, it seemed highly unlikely to Jensen that it would have gone unnoticed by Justin if Justin had in fact been playing on the fort.

Jensen couldn't put his finger on it yet, but

something kept bothering him. He felt as if Justin wasn't being totally honest with him about the events that occurred when Lee disappeared, but he didn't know why. He turned to Justin, and with a very solemn face told him that it was very important that he be as honest as he could be when relating the events surrounding his brother's disappearance. Justin responded that he was telling him the truth.

"Were you playing around or perhaps hiding from Lee before he disappeared?" asked Jensen.

"No, I wasn't," said Justin.

"If you've made up any part of this story because you're scared of what grown-ups might say to you, now is the time to tell me the complete truth so that we can look for your brother."

"But I am telling you the truth," insisted Justin. Justin, nervous and stammering, told Jensen that he ran home and told his father after discovering that his brother was missing. He was adamant that he hadn't seen any other adults at the playground besides the one he had described to Jensen and Officer Brown.

After taking Justin home, Jensen made arrangements that same evening to talk to Justin's friends, Mike Dobson and Ricky Stevens, in a conference room at Richmond School even though it was after hours. He talked to the boys separately to maintain the integrity of the interview.

Mike told the detective that when he and Ricky arrived at the playground, they observed that Justin and Lee were already there and were walking around the playground area. When he and Ricky started playing football, Justin joined in but Lee did not. After playing football for a while, Mike and Ricky went to another area of the playground to ride on their skateboards. Justin, however, stayed behind.

Mike said that at one point he looked toward the volcano where Lee had been playing, but Lee was no longer there. Instead he saw Lee walking by himself through the playground toward the gymnasium area, which Jensen knew to be westbound, and was soon out of sight. It was about two minutes later that Justin had asked him if he had seen his little brother, and Mike told him that Lee had just walked off. At that time Justin left the playground, and Mike and Ricky went to Ricky's house to have a snack and watch part of a movie. When they returned to the playground a short time later, they saw Justin and his father.

"Did you notice anyone else before you left? At about the time Lee walked off?" Jensen asked Mike.

"I think there were a couple of people in a pickup truck, in the front, you know, and three or four more people in the back," said Mike. "There was a dog back there, too."

"What kind of dog?"

"I think it was a German shepherd. The man and the dog got out of the back of the pickup, and the pickup left."

Mike described the man as Caucasian, in his thirties, approximately five feet ten inches to six feet tall with a medium build. He said he thought he remembered that the man had dark brown, somewhat wavy hair that extended over the collar. He was possibly wearing a down vest of some sort, light in color. He was also wearing a blue cap with a red "B" on the front which Mike described as being a Boston Red Sox hat. He also remembered that the man had a dark, short beard.

Mike couldn't tell Jensen specifically when the man was at the playground with the dog, or even if he had gone near the volcano where Lee was playing. Mike also couldn't remember if he saw the man before Lee disappeared, or if it had been some time afterward.

When Ricky Stevens came into the conference

room, he provided Jensen with a similar account of that Sunday's events. Justin and Lee were already on the playground, he said, and he thought that Justin was playing with a black male who appeared older, perhaps in the sixth or seventh grade. He remembered Lee playing on the volcano, and confirmed his friend's story about seeing the man get out of the back of a pickup truck with a German shepherd. He had little else that he could tell the detective, and Jensen went home that evening with a feeling of gloom in his gut. Something kept telling him that this was going to be a difficult case to solve, and that when he did solve it Lee Iseli would be dead.

Chapter Seven

Shortly after entering his apartment with Lee Iseli, Westley Allan Dodd sat the child down on his bed and took his photograph with the Polaroid camera, according to the entries Dodd made in his diary. He then brought out his briefcase from beneath the bed, unlocked and opened it, and took out his pink photo album labeled, "Family Memories." As he sat next to Lee on the bed, Dodd thumbed through the nude photos for the boy's benefit. Lee, however, exhibited only mild interest in the pictures.

After putting away the photo album, Dodd, speaking in a calm, quiet voice, instructed Lee to take off his clothes. Lee seemed to ignore him, and Dodd repeated the instructions while pulling off one of Lee's shoes. Dodd sensed a little resistance but removed Lee's other shoe and both of his socks, after which Lee pulled off his jacket and shirt. Dodd continued to coax the child to take off the rest of his clothes, and Lee pulled off his pants and Ghostbusters underpants in the same movement. Dodd immediately had Lee lay on his back on the bed and securely fastened the ropes, which he had preattached to each corner of the bed, to Lee's ankles and wrists. He then snapped the second photo and released Lee from the restraints.

Dodd removed his clothes, too, and for the next hour proceeded to molest Lee Iseli by performing oral sex on the boy. Afterward he allowed Lee to dress and wrote that "Lee's happy and cheerful." Together they watched Yogi Bear cartoons on television, after which Dodd placed the two photos of Lee inside his photo album.

"Do you want to spend the night with me?" asked Dodd at one point, feeling his way carefully.

"No, my brother might miss me," answered Lee without hesitation.

"Nah, your brother is probably having fun, too," retorted Dodd.

Dodd sat quietly in thought for a few moments, then added, "I'm sorry I don't have any toys for you to play with. Would you like to go to Kmart? I'll buy you a He-Man or a Robo-Cop toy, and then we can go to McDonald's for a burger if you'll spend the night with me." It was too much for Lee, or any child, to resist. He agreed.

While at Kmart Lee did the unexpected. He began thinking about his dad and brother again, and started crying. As Dodd attempted to calm him down, he kept saying that he wanted to go home. At one point Lee's pleas caught the attention of a store employee, and Dodd calmly explained that he was caring for his sister's child who wanted to go home but couldn't, not just yet, anyway. Dodd's explanation seemed to satisfy the store employee, after which Dodd selected and paid for a RoboCop toy. The toy helped calm Lee down, and they ate hamburgers together at McDonald's. Afterward Dodd allowed Lee a few minutes to play on the playground equipment outside the fast-food restaurant.

They were back inside Dodd's apartment by 6:30 P.M., and Lee continued to play with his new toy. Dodd, meanwhile, had already begun making plans to kill the boy. "He suspects nothing now," he wrote in his diary. "Will probably wait until morning to kill him. That way his body will still be fairly fresh for experiments after work. I'll suffocate him in his sleep when I wake up for work (if I sleep)."

When Lee grew tired of his toy, Dodd showed him his photo album again. Lee kept looking up at Dodd as he thumbed through the album, and at one point informed Dodd that he had to go to the bathroom. Dodd showed him where the bathroom was located, and later wrote how

114

he had "peeked through a crack in the door as he was taking a shit."

At approximately 9:00 P.M. Dodd showed Lee his photo album once more. It was, perhaps, an attempt by Dodd to sexually arouse himself before molesting the child again. Lee expressed some interest in seeing his own nude photos again, but made it clear to Dodd that he didn't want Dodd to take any more photos of him. "Little does he know," Dodd wrote, "that in about 20 hours I'll be taking photos of a dead, 4-year-old naked boy." By 9:45 P.M. Lee was in bed asleep, and by 10:00 P.M. Dodd had the boy, as well as himself, nude again.

Dodd "played" with Lee's genitals for the next hour while waiting for the 11:00 P.M. news, which was the first news broadcast since Lee "disappeared," and thought about ways in which he could kill him — "he'll either be choked, strangled, or suffocated. I don't want to leave marks on his neck but it must be quick and quiet." He decided that he would hide Lee's body on an upper shelf in the closet, and would conceal it by placing pillows and a sleeping bag in front of it "just in case the landlady decides to come in and have a look around" while Dodd was at work the next day.

Dodd didn't sleep at all that night. He was just too excited, overwhelmed by actually having a child inside his apartment. It was what he had been dreaming of and living for, and now it was a reality. And it had all been so very easy.

Dodd molested Lee throughout the night as he slept. At one point Lee woke up, but he was too tired and sleepy to pay much attention to what Dodd was doing to him. He apparently didn't mind or perhaps even notice that he was nude at 2:00 A.M., at which time Dodd pulled him up on top of him, "Lee's belly to mine, my cock in his crotch. He slept on top of me for half an hour as I rubbed his back and butt."

At 3:15 A.M. Lee woke up, at which time Dodd told him, "I'm going to kill you in the morning!"

"No, you're not!" said Lee, who then became frightened and started to cry. Before he began crying too loudly, Dodd tried to reassure him by telling him that he wouldn't really kill him. Lee apparently believed him and went back to sleep.

At 5:30 A.M. Dodd decided that it was time to kill Lee. As Lee lay sleeping on his back, Dodd crawled over him and positioned himself on Lee's left side and leaned into him, his body pinning Lee's right arm under a pillow. Holding Lee's left wrist with his left hand, Dodd had Lee totally pinned and he choked him with his right hand. Lee awoke and struggled violently, and managed to free his legs. Dodd tightened his grip on the boy's neck, but his hand became fatigued and he was forced to choke Lee with both of his hands. He tightly gripped Lee's throat for about fifteen seconds, until Lee ceased struggling and lay motionless.

Dodd waited about twenty seconds, then blew air into Lee's mouth one time to determine if he could be revived. At first it seemed as if he could not be revived, but twenty seconds later "he started slow gasps." Dodd choked him again, for approximately another minute until he lay still again. When Dodd released his grip, however, Lee began gasping for air again and opened his eyes. Dodd, by this time in a near frenzy, grabbed a rope that he kept by the bed and wrapped it around Lee's neck. Dodd tightened the rope and pulled the boy into an upright position with the ligature, and watched as Lee's chest heaved, unable to draw air into his lungs.

Holding the rope tight with his right hand, Dodd placed his other hand beneath Lee's buttocks and picked him up. He carried him to the clothes closet and held him up by just the rope with one hand while he moved the clothes on the clothes bar aside with the other. He then held Lee with his left hand as he tied the rope to the clothes bar, effectively hanging him "so I wouldn't get tired from the grip and maybe let him breathe again." Dodd left Lee hanging in the closet for about ten minutes while he cleaned up the room and snapped picture number seven with his Polaroid.

At 5:45 A.M. he cut the rope and lay the dead boy on the bed. He attempted to engage in postmortem oral sex with his victim, but soon gave up. He checked for a possible heartbeat and breathing, found neither, and placed Lee's body on the shelf in the closet behind pillows, blankets, and a sleeping bag. He then left for his job, vowing "I'll do more after work."

That evening Dodd read about the disappearance of Lee Iseli in *The Oregonian,* then sat down at his writing desk and caught up the entries in his diary:

4:50 p.m. Will now go take a leak and take the naked body of 4-year-old Lee Joseph Iseli out of the closet. I'll log everything as I go now. The paper article—labeled "The Oregonian, 10/30/89," was on page 5 of Section B, like it was no major deal he's missing. Looks like a perfect kidnapping.

5:05 p.m. Now getting Lee out of closet. Oh yeah—I knew for sure this morning he was dead. I'd heard of muscles relaxing and it's normal to "go potty" after dying — he peed on me twice as I hid his body in the closet, and once more on the shelf in the closet.

5:10 p.m. He is rather gross-looking — cold, stiff, and purple. . . .

5:16 p.m. See photos #8 and #9. . . . These photos show the position he's stuck in from being in a small closet area.

5:35 p.m. I'm going to go get some garbage bags now to put his bundled-up body into. Then I'll figure out a place to dump the "garbage." I'll wear gloves when handling the bags — no chance of fingerprints if someone discovers contents of the bag.

6:50 p.m. Now wearing gloves (after shower) to handle trash bags to put Lee in . . . washed his underwear in shower — Will now go dump his naked body.

8:00 p.m. Home. Dumped 7:35 p.m. on 10-30.

Chapter Eight

The following afternoon, Tuesday, October 31, Detective C. W. Jensen contacted Mark Prestwood, another of Justin Iseli's friends, whom he'd been unable to locate the day before. Although Mark had attended Richmond School with Justin, his family had recently moved, and he now attended Llewellyn School in the Sellwood area of Portland. It was at Llewellyn School that Jensen interviewed him.

Mark told Jensen that he had known Justin and Lee for approximately four months. On Sunday, October 29, Mark said he went to the Iselis' house, and he and Justin soon decided to go to Richmond School. As was their custom, they took Lee with them.

"Justin is always in charge of his little brother," said Mark. He described how they walked to the school, and his story matched Justin's until he got to the part where he left the school to go and get another of their friends, Tim Fisher,* who lived near Forty-ninth Avenue and Clinton Street. As he started to leave the school, he said, Lee Iseli began to follow him until Justin stopped him. That was the last time he saw Lee.

On the way to Tim's house, however, he had seen a strange man. He said the man was white, in his thirties, had dark hair and a beard, a tan jacket, and white pants. The man was not wearing a hat. Mark thought the man was strange because he was talking to himself. Shortly after he arrived at Tim's house, Mark and Tim returned to the school yard and saw the same strange man along the way, this time with a large shaggy orange-colored dog. Mark said that he thought the man was singing to himself about wearing thermal underwear, which only added to his "strangeness."

Upon arrival at the school, Mark said, both boys observed Justin as he exited a large tan pickup truck with red pin stripes. The truck was driven by a white male with dark hair. It was at that time that Justin told Mark that his brother was missing.

Jensen wondered, why hadn't Justin mentioned the fact that Lee had attempted to follow Mark away from the school grounds when Mark went to get Tim? And why hadn't he mentioned being inside a large tan pickup truck? Jensen couldn't help but think about the omissions, and decided that the only way he would be able to determine if they had any bearing on the case was to reinterview Justin.

When Jensen met again with Justin at his home, he told the boy that some of his previous statements did not agree with what other people were telling him and the other police officers. Jensen said he was also troubled by the fact that employees of the Kienow's store had seen Lee alone inside the store looking at candy on aisle seven *after* Justin said he saw his brother talking to the man at the school. Even though Jensen thought it was possible that Lee had wandered away from the playground on his own, he couldn't reconcile that possibility with Justin's story of having last seen Lee on the volcano at 1:00 P.M.

Although Justin continued to maintain that he had last seen Lee on the volcano, he told Jensen that Lee had wanted to go inside the store when they walked past it earlier on their way to the school playground. However, he hadn't allowed Lee to go inside, and insisted that neither he nor Lee had gone inside the store. When asked whether he had gone to a stranger for help in finding Lee, Justin denied that anyone had helped him. At that point, however, Justin admitted that he had initially lied about being on the playground structure known as the fort when Lee disappeared.

"Okay, Justin," said Jensen, becoming more frustrated but trying not to let it show, "why don't you just start all over and tell me what actually occurred at the school playground."

After a few moments of nervous silence, Justin began again by stating that he had been playing football with his friends on the paved portion of the playground, an area near the fort and the volcano. Lee came over and talked briefly to Justin, then went to the volcano to play by himself. In the meantime Justin had gone with his friends to another part of the playground, but was still nearby. At that time, he said, he noticed that a stranger was talking to Lee at the volcano. However, he admitted, he had not, as he had previously told Jensen, gone over to Lee to tell him not to talk to strangers. Instead he had remained with his friends and sat on top of a garbage can, his back turned to Lee. Five minutes later he looked around toward the volcano and noticed that Lee was gone.

After noticing that Lee had disappeared, Justin ran around the playground and school building in search of him. Unable to find his brother anywhere, he saw a man, in a tan pickup truck, who apparently had noticed that he was looking for someone. The man asked him if he needed assistance, and when Justin explained what had happened the man told him to get inside the truck and that he would help him. They spent the next several minutes driving around the school and adjacent neighborhood looking for Lee. Unable to find Lee, the man drove Justin to his home, taking the same route that Justin always took to and from school because that was the route that Lee also knew.

"How do you think Lee could have disappeared while you were only a short distance away from him?" asked Jensen.

"I had my back towards him, and so did my friends," said Justin, occasionally stammering and obviously distraught over his brother's disappearance. Although Jensen didn't know it yet, Justin's latest version of the events would be consistent with what Westley Allan Dodd wrote in his diary about the abduction.

As Justin continued relating what had happened, he told Jensen that Lee would believe just about anything that anybody would tell him. In childlike speculation, Justin theorized that the strange man he had seen talking to Lee may have simply told Lee that his brother had left the playground. Justin figured that Lee probably would have believed the man and would have gone with him to look for Justin.

"Why wouldn't Lee simply have looked where he knew you were sitting by the garbage can with your back to him?" asked Jensen.

"Lee just wouldn't. Besides, Lee wouldn't recognize me from the back."

At another point in the interview, Jensen described a hypothetical situation to Justin in an attempt to explain why Lee had been seen in the Kienow's store.

"Is it possible that you sent Lee into the store to get something for you?" asked Jensen.

"No," answered Justin. After a few moments, however, Justin admitted that he had suggested to Lee that he go to the store. "I halfway think Lee went to the store and that I may have sent him in."

Justin then described a "game" in which he had jokingly told Lee to go to the Kienow's store. He said that he was still sitting on the garbage can on the playground at the time, and described how he and Lee sometimes took separate routes to get to the same place. He said that he jokingly told Lee to meet him at the store, after which he went through the motions of pretending to run around the east side of the school toward the store while Lee ran west around the other side of the building. Justin said that he yelled at Lee at one point to try and stop him, but Lee was already out of sight by that time. Justin said that he sat around for about "two minutes" before deciding to run around the school in an attempt to find Lee. He admitted that there was no strange man in the area of the volcano at that time, but stated that a man had walked by that area a little earlier and had said "Hi" to them but had continued walking on through the playground.

After running around the school and unable to find Lee, Justin said he ran to the Kienow's store and peered in through the doors and windows. However, he did not see Lee inside the store and immediately returned to the school where he met the man, who had helped him in the tan pickup.

"Where were your friends while you were playing this game with Lee?" asked Jensen.

"They had already left."

"Why did you feel like you had to make up the original stories about the incident?"

"I felt stupid, and didn't want to be blamed."

Jensen felt that Justin's latest explanation was the truth, and that it cleared up a few things. It explained, Jensen felt, why the tracking dogs had picked up Lee's scent from the school to the store, and why store employees had reported seeing Lee inside the store. It also helped explain why the tracking dogs had picked up his scent at the school but had abruptly lost it at the curb on Sherman Street. Jensen theorized that while Justin was at the store looking for Lee, Lee had already gone back to the playground. They had missed each other, he believed, by only a couple of minutes, perhaps by taking slightly different routes around the school building. By the time Justin had returned to the school, Lee had already been abducted. Jensen now believed that Lee had gotten into a car, either of his own will or by force, parked along Sherman Street.

When Jensen related the latest turn of events to his colleagues, he said he believed that Justin's earlier version of what happened was the result of trauma from feeling responsible for losing his brother.

"He was simply scared," said Jensen. "He was so scared that he had done something wrong, when in reality, of course, he hadn't."

That same day a female resident of the Southeast Portland neighborhood from which Lee Iseli had disappeared reported to police several strange encounters that she'd had with a man who lived nearby. According to the report, the woman had been a witness against the man in a civil matter several months earlier. The man, she said, apparently had held a grudge against her because he had consistently harassed her and her children ever since she testified against him. She said she was only reporting the problem now because she had been stirred up and disturbed by Lee Iseli's disappearance and wondered whether the man might have had something to do with the abduction.

Two months earlier, the woman told the police, she received a package in her mailbox. It was addressed to her and, although it had postage stamps on it, the stamps had not been canceled by the post office. Instead of the official cancelation, the stamps had several pen strokes drawn through them.

When she opened the package, she found a large piece of sausage that was beginning to mildew. It was approximately eight to ten inches long, and had been carefully carved into the shape of an erect human penis. The package had arrived at a time when tension between the woman and the man was at its highest. The man, police learned, had since moved away, and they had not been able to immediately locate him. Although they didn't have any reason to believe that he had been involved in Lee Iseli's disappearance, they couldn't completely ignore such a possibility considering the strange circumstances between him and the woman. The report was filed with Jensen's ever-growing list of sex offenders and perverts known in the area, and the individual would be looked at carefully when it came time to begin screening and prioritizing the names on the list.

In another incident a motorist driving along Southeast Thirty-ninth Avenue reported to police that she had seen a boy matching Lee Iseli's description near Hawthorne Street. The child was crying and was obviously distraught. An old bag lady, with all of her worldly possessions parked nearby in a shopping cart, appeared to be trying to comfort him. However, when Portland officers assigned to that area tracked the bag lady down, she told them that she didn't recall any instances in which she had spoken to a young boy.

In the same locale during the same time frame, another motorist reported seeing a man struggling with a young child matching Lee's description; the man had appeared to be attempting to force him inside a car. The witness could not tell if the boy was the man's son or not, but something about the exchange, namely the adult's reported pleading and yelling, seemed to indicate to investigating officers that the man and boy were related. Even though it didn't seem quite like an abduction, the report was filed with other reports of suspicious activities surrounding the Lee Iseli case.

Perhaps one of the most chilling reports in that category was called in by Ricky Stevens's mother, who of course knew Lee and Justin personally because they were friends with her son. Leona Stevens* called East Precinct to report that she had experienced a "vision" while she was driving home a day earlier, on Monday, October 30. She stated that the "vision" depicted Lee Iseli in bright white. He was either clothed in white or was naked, she said, and was lying facedown in black mud beside a body of water. She saw black leaves and branches in the "vision," and there appeared to be bushes nearby. She told the officer that her teenage daughter dreamed that same night that Lee Iseli had died. She could not "see" the suspect or the suspect's vehicle in her premonition, but added that she often experienced premonitions that repeatedly proved to be true. She said she had told several people about the premonition, but people usually didn't pay her much credence.

Whether or not any of the bizarre series of incidents had any factual bearing on the Lee Iseli investigation, of course, remained to be seen. The investigators just had no way of knowing yet whether any of the information would help them determine what had happened to Lee. But all of the reports had to be looked into, at least until they had a suspect they could focus on exclusively. Such reports went on and on, and kept Jensen and his colleagues busier than they had been in months checking all of them out. They were soon working twelve-hour days, literally living and breathing the Lee Iseli case.

By the evening of Halloween Night, the Portland Police Bureau reluctantly began to scale back the scope of their search efforts, though the investigative efforts continued with great intensity. A second search of all of the area's parks and playgrounds with Mountain Wilderness Dogs had failed to turn up any sign of Lee, and intensive door-to-door canvassing of the neighborhoods had failed to generate any new leads. Barring any unusual developments, there simply weren't any other likely places to search for the child. Although the police had privately expressed their fear that Lee had been abducted, they began saying so publicly at that point.

"There doesn't seem to be any other explanation," said Sergeant Terry Gray. "You can rack your brain, but you can't think of what a four-year-old boy would be doing all this time. I can't think of any other possible excuse. If he was staying with a friend somewhere, I'm sure the parents would have called by now. They must know he's missing."

Even though it was Halloween, the holiday for children, it just wasn't the same in Lee Iseli's neighborhood. The spirit of the night was markedly dampened as more parents than usual accompanied their children from house to house, obviously a result of their fear for their own children's safety in the aftermath of Lee's unexplained disappearance. Lee, a big fan of the *Ghostbusters* movies and cartoon series, had been looking forward to wearing his Ghostbusters costume that Halloween. But the costume went unused, and the friends he would have gone trick or treating with were very much aware of his absence. Many children said they missed him, and some openly cried because of the uncertainty of what had become of the boy.

Lee's father theorized, in hope against hope, that perhaps a lonely adult had abducted his boy and was taking care of him. He made a public plea to anyone holding Lee to release him.

"There are a lot of people out there who are lonely," said Iseli. "Maybe someone who never had a child or who never got to dress up on Halloween or never got presents at Christmas (is holding Lee). If it's someone like that, he could just drop him off at a store or street corner." Sadly, Bob Iseli's plea went unheeded. Even if Westley Allan Dodd had heard his plea and had wanted to return Lee to his home, there was no way that he could. Lee was already dead.

In the meantime, as useless clues continued to pour in and create more work for the overburdened investigators, a reporter for *The Oregonian* newspaper contacted Detective David W. Simpson of the Portland Police Bureau concerning a letter he had received anonymously regarding satanic cult activity in Southeast Portland. The writer of the letter stated that the cult activity could be related to the disappearance of Lee Iseli, and would be one more item to be added to the case's suspicious activities file.

The letter, dated October 31, 1989, was an obvious photocopy. The reporter told Simpson that it had been handled only by himself and one other person. After Multnomah County Deputy District Attorney Norm Frink read the letter, it was turned over to Detective Jensen who requested that the Bureau's Identification Division process it for fingerprints. The letter's text is as follows:

Re: Tip. A possible connection between the suspected kidnapping of Lee Eisley (sic), a child aged 4 on the day of the Black Mass and Spiral Dance held by the Portland community of witches and satanists that night within a few blocks of the abduction.

Last Sunday afternoon, according to news reports, a small 4 year old child, Lee Eisley (sic) may have been abducted from the Keinow's (sic) store near S.E. 39th and Division. The boy is described as weighing approx. 30 pounds and standing 3 plus feet tall and having a shock of blond hair over his eyes. This little boy had been accompanied by his 9-year-old brother, both children of a single father. This abduction may have taken place around 1:00 pm on the afternoon of Sunday Oct. 29, 1989. As of the date of this letter, he has not been located and the non-custodial parent, his Mother, denies taking him.

(The above information was taken from local radio news reports.)

ADDITIONAL INFORMATION

On the night of this same day, Sunday, October 29, 1989, 50 to 70 of Portland's Satanist community, witches and practitioners of the occult gathered to celebrate what they call "The Spiral Dance" and Black

Mass at the Echo Theater located at 1515 S.E. 37th (37th and Hawthorne).

This celebration of the occult began at approx. 6:45 pm and the last of the Satanists departed the premises at approx. 11:00 pm. These people both male and female and some dressed in "drag" were observed by witnesses wearing all manner of black occult traditional garb: black masks, witch hats, and black dresses and some were dressed in only street clothes.

There was a black curtain over the window which was occasionally drawn slightly so that a large pentagram could be seen suspended from the ceiling with streamers hanging down, presumably as accessories to the spiral dance. A Black Mass was also held.

It is notable that all satanists had departed by 11:00 pm, perhaps to attend another "event" at another location at midnight. (?)

The writer of the letter also included several vehicle license plate numbers and identifications parked at or near the theater at the time the purported "Spiral Dance" and "Black Mass" occurred. The writer also noted a number of bumper stickers, including, "Keep Abortion Legal"; a Jewish Star of David with the phrasing, "One Love, One People, One Destiny"; another that read, "This is the season of the witch"; "Sing back the buffalo and swan"; and "My other car is a broom." The writer also urged the reporter to contact a declared witch, who was named in the text along with a telephone number. The remainder of the letter's text is as follows:

One would have to be extremely naive and blind not to see a possible connection, at least worth checking out between the disappearance of the young boy Lee Eisley (sic), and the satanists. Every Halloween children disappear all over the country and are murdered by this human garbage. It is irresponsible of the Portland Police to not have a detective on these people at all times as the rise of Satanic occultism is a growing national problem. It would seem to some, that the close proximity to the Echo Theater and the Keinow's (sic) store would be too obvious, but not if one wanted to get the child out of sight quickly. Also, criminals in Portland are becoming less and less respecting or afraid of the police authorities, so what's another murder.

We are submitting this anonymously because we can trust neither the Satanists or the police.

The report from the Identification Division showed that there were three fingerprints on the letter: two were from people at *The Oregonian* and another belonged to Deputy District Attorney Norman Frink, who had inadvertently touched a corner of the document while reading it. Whoever typed and photocopied the letter had taken extreme caution to avoid leaving his or her fingerprints on it, and Jensen, at this point, had no leads to the writer's identity or to Lee Iseli's whereabouts. Jensen would ultimately learn that neither the letter nor the satanic group had any direct bearing on the case, but not for another two weeks.

That same evening in Vancouver, Washington, Westley Allan Dodd had watched the evening news and had seen the composite drawing of the man seen talking to Lee at the school. He noted in his diary that it "looked a lot like me." He listened with great interest as the news anchor said that the "person of interest" was wearing a blue baseball cap when seen and may have had a German shepherd with him when he exited a pickup truck. After hearing that the FBI had entered the case, Dodd decided that he would watch the news carefully for the next month or so and remain out of sight.

Dodd carefully gathered up Lee's socks, shirt, sweater, and pants; placed them inside a sack; and burned them inside a trash burning barrel outside the duplex in the backyard. When he returned to his apartment, he took Lee's shoes; cut them into four pieces; placed them inside two sacks; and burned them, too, along with newspapers from which he had clipped articles about Lee's disappearance. He kept the articles that he had cut out, however, as well as Lee's Ghostbuster underpants for souvenirs, and hid them inside his briefcase next to his "Family Memories" photo album.

Chapter Nine

Early the next morning, Wednesday, November 1, 1989, sixty-seven-year-old St. Elmo Abernathy left his Southeast Portland home and drove a few miles north on Interstate 5 to Vancouver, Washington. He was going pheasant hunting at the Washington State Game Preserve, located near Vancouver Lake at the end of La Frambois Road. Abernathy had been there before, and he knew the hunting to be good due to the fact that the Washington State Department of Wildlife stocked the preserve twice weekly with pheasant during hunting season. He couldn't have been in a better mood as he exited the freeway, passed through part of Vancouver, turned onto La Frambois Road, and drove down the two-mile, two-lane asphalt road. A few minutes later he passed through the entrance to the game preserve.

It was 8:00 A.M. when he pulled his truck into the first parking area, made up of small aggregate base rock and located adjacent to the lake's south shore. There was also a second parking lot, often referred to as the north parking lot, made up of larger two-inch aggregate rock. But Abernathy always parked in the first lot, as if it were part of his territory and marked for his use. He parked near the lake's boat ramp and quickly unloaded his gun and a small backpack. His bird dog jumped out of the back of his truck.

Abernathy and his dog walked slowly out of the lakeside parking lot, surrounded on three sides by tall grass, large boulders and trees, through an open gate at the northwest corner of the lot and entered into an expanse of the tall grass and brush. The area, circumscribed by farm land and orchards, was isolated from the city and residential areas and seemed rife for hunting birds that morning, just as it had been on Abernathy's previous hunting trips there.

However, after beating about the brush for his quarry for the next hour and a half, Abernathy realized that the hunting wasn't anywhere nearly as good as he had first thought it would be. Other hunters must have gotten there early, perhaps at 4:00 A.M. when the preserve officially opened for the day. After deciding to call it quits, at least for that day, he whistled for his dog and together they began walking back toward the parking lot. He had walked only a few yards on the return trip when he noticed a lily-white object in the brush just ahead of him. He squinted his eyes but still couldn't quite make out what it was. It looked almost like a large, lifelike doll, but he couldn't believe that someone would have discarded something like that out there. Abernathy, now more than a little curious, continued to approach it, with his dog taking the lead. When he was within five feet of the object, the dog ran the rest of the way over and sniffed at it. Abernathy suddenly stopped dead in his tracks and stared in horror at the object in front of him.

"Oh shit!" he said to himself when he realized that what he'd stumbled upon was not a doll. It was a human—a dead little boy. Without calling out to any of the other hunters in the area, Abernathy returned to his truck and attempted to raise someone on Channel 9 of his CB radio. Unsuccessful, he loaded his dog into the bed of the pickup and drove to the nearest telephone, which was located a few miles away at a deli on Thirty-ninth Street and Fruit Valley Road. With trembling hands he dialed 911 and reported his grim discovery to the Clark County Sheriff's Department. A dispatcher took the details and advised him to wait at the deli until a deputy arrived.

Deputy Dave Lundy, who officially would be the first officer on the scene, arrived at the deli's parking lot at 9:51 A.M. Abernathy saw the deputy and immediately went over to him. The distraught, tearful hunter recounted how he had nearly stumbled onto the dead, naked little boy and where he had found him. Lundy followed him to the game preserve.

Abernathy led Lundy to an area situated between the first and second parking lots. After very little searching, Abernathy easily found the body again, lying in a bushy area approximately seventy-five feet south of the north parking lot and approximately fifty feet west of La Frambois Road. Lundy, who remained a good distance away from the body to avoid inadvertently contaminating the crime scene, could see that the body was indeed that of a small male child, unclothed and lying on his back. His head was oriented to the east and his right foot was oriented to the northwest. His legs were spread apart, exposing his genitalia, and it appeared that his body was covered with debris. It was obvious to Lundy that no attempt had been made to conceal the body, and he could see no clothing anywhere near the corpse. As they backed away from the area to preserve any evidence that might be present, Lundy asked Abernathy to explain the circumstances surrounding his discovery of the body.

"When I got there," said Abernathy, "there were probably twenty-five people going in to hunt. At 8:00 A.M. we all started walking through the fields." He explained that he and the others split up at one point, and when he finished hunting an hour and a half later he found the body on the way back to his truck.

"I was coming back to the parking lot," said Abernathy. "And there it was. I thought it was a doll at first, and my dog went over and smelled it. Then I saw that it had a little peter and I knew that it was real. I was shocked . . . that someone would do that . . . and put a little dead boy out there. It's the worst thing I've ever seen in my life."

Deputy Lundy called in his report of a homicide to Detective Sergeant Bob Rayburn, who in turn notified his boss, Lieutenant James Pillsbury. As a result, Detectives Dave Trimble and Rick Buckner caught the assignment, and they arrived at the remote location accompanied by their shift supervisor, Sergeant Mike Kestner, at 10:20 A.M. It was an assignment that would haunt them, and everyone else associated with the case, for the rest of their lives.

Before another half hour passed, the game preserve was literally crawling with law officers. By then Sheriff Frank Kanekoa, uncle to Captain Bob Kanekoa of the Vancouver Police Department, and Undersheriff Bob Songer had arrived, as had Clark County Coroner Archie Hamilton and Prosecutor Art Curtis. Because a child was involved and because it was possible that the case might be related to the Neer brothers' murders, Detective Jeff Sundby and several of his colleagues from the Vancouver Police Department were summoned to the scene even though the Vancouver Lake area was outside the city limits and not in their jurisdiction.

Detectives Trimble and Buckner observed two distinct paths which led to the boy's body. One of the paths led from the direction of the road and the other from the direction of the parking lots. Because St. Elmo Abernathy had approached from the direction of the parking lots, the detectives theorized that whoever dumped the body at the location had parked on the road some fifty feet away. Accompanied by Deputy Lundy, Trimble and Buckner approached the body from the area they considered to be the least likely path used by the perpetrator.

When Trimble got within fifteen feet of the

body, he told his colleagues that it appeared to be the corpse of the missing Portland boy, Lee Iseli. He couldn't be certain, he said as he returned the same way he had come, but it looked like the photographs he had seen of Lee. At 10:26 A.M. Sergeant Rayburn contacted C.W. Jensen of the Portland Police Bureau. Jensen advised Rayburn that he and Detective Dave Rubey, who had recently been assigned to work the case with Jensen, would be there in short order.

While waiting for Jensen and Rubey to arrive, Detective Buckner approached the body using the same path that Trimble had used. From approximately fifteen feet away, Buckner, like his partner, observed that the body was that of a white male, approximately four to five years old. His hair was blond, and he was lying in an area where the grass was two to three feet high. He, too, believed that the body was that of the missing Portland boy. Buckner, however, noticed a reddish discoloration on the victim's neck and at first thought that his throat might have been cut. But when he approached a little closer, he could see that the discoloration looked more like a ligature mark.

Jensen and Rubey attempted to prepare

145

themselves mentally for the crime scene while they were en route, like they did with all of their homicide cases. When they arrived at the crime scene at 11:01 A.M., all it took was one look at the body for each to know that no amount of mental preparation would have helped them with this one. Seeing the child's naked body discarded like garbage was too much for even the most callous of cops to take. Despite the intense feelings of dread, anger, and sadness that pulsed and flickered back and forth between his mind and his heart, Jensen, holding a black and white photograph of Lee Iseli, sullenly approached the body.

When he was within a few feet of the corpse, all the while maintaining a safe distance to preserve unseen evidence, he compared its face with the photograph in his hand. The eyes of the dead boy on the ground in front of him were closed; the hair was rumpled; the mouth was closed; and the skin had the deathly purple hue that Jensen had seen so many times before. Even though it was in stark contrast to the two-dimensional smiling, spirited face he held in his hand, Jensen felt certain that he was looking down at the murdered body of Lee Iseli. Recalling that Lee's father had told him that Lee had been fingerprinted a few weeks earlier, Jensen made arrangements to obtain

Lee's fingerprint card for comparison, just to be sure.

According to Coroner Archie Hamilton, the body was cold to the touch and covered with grass, leaves, and other debris. He noted discoloration of the lips and what appeared to be dried blood inside the left nostril. There appeared to be ligature marks around the victim's wrists, ankles, and throat. Hamilton made no attempt to open the boy's closed eyes at the scene to check for petechial hemorrhaging, common in strangulation victims. That could be done later, at the time of autopsy. Because the vegetation directly beneath the body was knocked down, with the tops of the grass pointing in a southwesterly direction, it appeared to everyone present that the perpetrator had thrown the body into the area from a distance, tossed there like rubbish as opposed to being deposited there gently. It was but another grim fact that allowed the homicide probers a glimpse into the mind of the killer they hunted.

Because the case appeared to be multi-jurisdictional, the Vancouver Police Department, Portland Police Bureau, and the Clark County Sheriff's Department consulted with one another to determine which agency would conduct the processing of the crime scene for evidence. Because the body was discovered in Clark

County, all of the officials agreed that the task should be accomplished by the Clark County Sheriff's Department. However, because everyone believed that a serial child killer could be involved, a task force was promptly formed with investigators from all of the agencies concerned.

Sergeant Craig Hogman, evidence technician for the Clark County Sheriff's Department, and Detective Melanie Kenoyer were assigned the duties of conducting the crime scene search and processing. Prior to removing the body, Hogman and Kenoyer photographed, measured, and collected trace evidence on and around the corpse. A baseline was used to take the measurements, and after they were completed Deputy Coroner Russ Smith entered the crime scene to remove the body. After wrapping the body in a plain white sheet that afternoon, Smith had the corpse taken to the Multnomah County Medical Examiner's office in Portland, the nearest morgue facility where an autopsy could be conducted.

After the body was removed, Hogman and Kenoyer proceeded to conduct an inch-by-inch search of the area where the body had lain. Using stakes and twine, they completed a grid pattern consisting of 122 quadrants from where the body had lain and extended outward from that point. Officers from the Portland Police Bureau, Mountain Wilderness Search Dog Rescue, Washington State Police Explorers, Silver Star Search and Rescue, Clark County Search and Rescue, and the Clark County Explorers and Reserves took part in the search for evidence. Anything that wasn't a part of the natural setting, items such as trash, cigarette butts, a condom, clothing, rope, and so forth, was marked off, photographed, and collected as evidence. By the time they had completed their search of all the quadrants in the grid, however, they failed to find any clothing that might have belonged to the victim. Before leaving the area, Hogman made one additional search using a metal detector, but found nothing else of evidentiary value.

That same day, the body found at the game preserve was positively identified as Lee Joseph Iseli by John Kruse and Stan Sterba of the Portland Police Bureau's Identification Division. The positive identification was based on fingerprints that were obtained from Lee's father, who had Lee fingerprinted a few months earlier at a children's fair in Portland.

Portland Police Bureau Detectives Mike Hefley and Tom Nelson were standing by, ready to deliver the tragic news to Lee's family when the identification was made in as sensitive a manner as was humanly possible. They also arranged for volunteer chaplain Elaine Caldwell to accompany them to the Iseli residence, and for officers to pick Justin up at Richmond School so that he, too, would be home when the crushing news was delivered. When they arrived, however, they found that a reporter for *The Oregonian* had already contacted Robert Iseli and had attempted to get his reaction to the discovery of the child's body found in Vancouver before word of the positive identification had been relayed by the police to Lee's father.

When Hefley and Nelson were invited into the house, Iseli took them upstairs and explained that he wanted to talk to them out of earshot of his mother and grandmother. He said that his grandmother had a severe heart condition and he was concerned that she might suffer a heart attack from the shock of bad news. When the detectives informed him that the news was indeed bad, Iseli lowered his head and appeared quiet, subdued for a few moments. Then he spoke.

"If you find the guy, keep him away from

me. A lot of people would like to kill him."

Later that afternoon Dr. Larry Lewman, Oregon State Medical Examiner, performed a definitive autopsy on Lee Iseli's body and concluded that the child had died as a result of strangulation. Although the autopsy did not determine conclusively how long Lee had been dead when his body was discovered, mild decomposition was noted in the area of his stomach and indicated that he had been dead for at least a day, perhaps two. In addition to the neck and wrists, Lewman noted that a ligature mark was present around Lee's left ankle. Lewman believed that twine or rope had been used to strangle and bind the child.

Dr. Jan Bays, an attending physician brought in to help determine if Lee had been sexually assaulted, examined the child's genitalia and anus. Although there was no obvious blood in the anus, there was "mucoid material" and "fecal soiling." The boy's anus was gaping, and Dr. Bays found three lacerations that were visible. When specimens of the anus and lower rectum were dyed and examined under the colposcope, Dr. Bays found fifteen additional lacerations. The findings, said the doctor, confirmed anal penetration. Lee had been sodomized.

As a panicked community started to talk and rumors began to fly, authorities from all of the police departments involved attempted to play down any possible connection between Lee Iseli's murder and the stabbing deaths of Billy and Cole Neer nearly two months earlier. Publicly, the investigators said that the killer's method of operation was different in the Iseli case. They quickly pointed out that Lee had been strangled and that Billy and Cole had been stabbed repeatedly. Archie Hamilton, the Clark County Coroner, bolstered that declaration by stating that there were "absolutely no similarities at this point" in the two cases. Privately, however, the detectives felt that there might be a connection.

Detective David Simpson of the Portland Police Bureau was one of those who believed there might be a connection, and he said so. He didn't want parents, nor did any of the other law officers, to let their guard down while the killer was still at large. He didn't want to cause a widespread panic, either, so he was somewhat guarded in his public remarks.

"I'd like to say it's an isolated incident, but I don't say it reassuringly," said Simpson. "We don't know enough yet about what happened. But I think we as a community need to be extremely cautious until we get more answers."

He added that this was the first case of its type in the area.

"We're up to our elbows in alligators trying to get this case to make some sense," added Undersheriff Robert Songer. "Just that a four-year-old child was murdered doesn't make sense to begin with. What could a four-year-old do to make someone kill him?"

Meanwhile, a psychologist specializing in sexual abuse and homicide cases provided the detectives with a likely profile of Lee Iseli's killer. The psychologist told the probers that their killer was probably a middle-class or blue-collar working man who had often fantasized about killing a child. The killer was probably living a pretty normal life-style, but was harboring a tremendous amount of hostility.

"The killer has been having thoughts like this for a long period of time," said the psychologist. "I would assume that he has fantasized about this type of behavior . . . the other possibility is that this could be a drug-crazed individual, but I think that would be pretty unusual. The person probably leads a passive life and finally had to act this out."

"It's hard to say or even look at someone and say, 'This is a child killer,'" countered

Clark County Sheriff Frank Kanekoa. "I have a hard time handling a case where a child of any age is murdered in this fashion. I can't fathom the thinking of someone who would hurt a child who can't do anyone any harm. It's too early in the case to say. We need to gather more evidence before we come out with a profile."

Despite a telephone hot line and a ten-thousand-dollar reward fund, a monster continued to walk the community's streets while frustrated detectives quickly ran out of leads.

Chapter Ten

The next afternoon, Thursday, November 2, Portland Police Bureau Officer C.R. Wooden-Johnson and a number of other officers were sent out to again canvass the Southeast Portland neighborhood where Lee Iseli had lived. By then the Portland office of the FBI had joined in on the effort since it was official that Lee had been kidnapped, transported across a state line, and murdered. Much of the work was routine. Officers and agents knocked on doors, showed a photograph of Lee, and asked if anyone had seen him on the day he was abducted. In many instances residents acknowledged that they had known Lee and had seen him, both by himself and with friends and his brother, in the neighborhood often. However, it wasn't until Officer Wooden-Johnson knocked on a door at a house in the 2500 block of Southeast Forty-third Avenue that anything significant was learned.

A twelve-year-old girl, Cathy Evans,* came to the door and told Wooden-Johnson that one of her friends, Paula Finch,* lived directly across the street from Richmond School and had told her something that she felt was important in connection with the Lee Iseli case. Cathy said that Paula had told her about having seen a yellow car in front of Richmond School on the day that Lee disappeared, and had later seen a young blond boy who looked very much like Lee sitting in that same car with an adult male. She hadn't thought much about it at the time, and never thought anything about it until after Lee's abduction and murder had become public knowledge.

Unfortunately, when Wooden-Johnson talked with Paula Finch she had little more to offer him than what her friend had reported. She hadn't obtained the car's license plate number, and didn't know the make and model. She also hadn't obtained a good enough look at the driver to be able to describe him. Even though the information was written up in a report, it was just another good lead that had dead ended just like most of the others.

Nearby, in the same neighborhood but on a different street, FBI Special Agent Steven E. Warner was responsible for canvassing Division Street. He wasn't having much luck finding anyone who had known Lee until he stopped at a flower shop near Thirty-second and Division and spoke to co-owner David Nelson.* Nelson, who told Warner that he was quite familiar with the boy's kidnapping and murder from all of the media attention that the case was receiving, had known Lee quite well. Nelson characterized Lee as the little boy who followed his older brother everywhere, and said that they seemed inseparable during the summer months. However, after school started in September, Lee was often seen in the neighborhood by himself.

Lee sometimes stopped by the flower shop to talk to Nelson, who always enjoyed the boy's visits, but Lee was more interested in playing with Nelson's pet dog than in talking to him. Lee seemed fascinated with dogs, as most kids his age would be, he said. Nelson described Lee as a somewhat boisterous kid but with a sunny disposition who made friends easily. On a few occasions Lee would stay for several hours watching Nelson as he conducted business and prepared flower arrangements, always playing with the dog. Nelson recalled one instance in which Lee had stayed for four hours. He finally had to send him home, but half an hour later Lee returned, acting big and talking in a "grown-up" voice. He was such a beautiful kid, and Nelson just couldn't understand how anyone could have killed him, let alone kill any child.

He said the last time he had seen Lee was on the Wednesday before the abduction.

"Lee was my little buddy," said Nelson. "He was a sweet little kid, everybody's friend. I'm sure gonna miss him."

While the neighborhood canvass was underway, the search for the man associated with a pickup truck and a German shepherd dog was stepped up. His description, as provided by Justin Iseli and two of his friends, had appeared in the newspaper that day and was being broadcast on most of the television and radio news reports. Detective C.W. Jensen and his colleagues wanted very much to talk with the man, either to eliminate him as a suspect or to intensify their focus on him. Unfortunately, they had no leads to his identity.

Meanwhile, Portland Detectives Jensen and Rubey met with Clark County Detectives Trimble and Buckner at Portland's Detective Division, located downtown in the Justice Center. It was decided by their superiors at that time that they would lead the task force, and that Jensen and Trimble would work as partners. The Portland Police Bureau and the Clark County Sheriff's Department would work together, along with their colleagues at the Vancouver Police

Department, to hopefully solve Lee Iseli's murder. Even though the homicide had occurred in Clark County, it was decided that the detectives would work together as a unit based at the Justice Center. Logistically it seemed like the best place to work, particularly since the Oregon State Police Crime Laboratory was located in the same building.

Shortly after 5:00 P.M., while the detectives were making duplicates of all of the police reports generated by each agency so that they could share them with each other, Jensen received a telephone call from a man who identified himself as Brad Perkins.* Jensen listened intently while Perkins explained that he had just returned from the Rolling Stones concert, held on November 1 in Vancouver, British Columbia, and had been reading newspaper accounts of Lee Iseli's abduction and murder when he suddenly realized that he was the man with the German shepherd they were looking for. He gave Jensen his address and said that he wanted to clear up the matter as soon as possible. Jensen told him that he felt likewise, and assured Perkins that he and his partner would be right out.

Jensen and Trimble wondered, was this their first major break in the case? It was definitely too good to be true, they felt; incredible, really, that this individual had come forward voluntarily. The two detectives dropped what they were doing and left their colleagues in charge of the photocopying. They departed for Perkins's residence, located in the 1900 block of Southeast Forty-seventh Avenue, almost immediately.

When Jensen and Trimble arrived, Perkins calmly explained that he and his wife, accompanied by a neighbor, had driven to the area of Richmond School on Sunday afternoon, October 29. The school, he said, was near a building that was being vacated by his wife's employer. His wife was going to that building to determine the extent of cleanup work that would be needed. She was driving their Datsun pickup, their neighbor was sitting in the passenger seat, and Perkins and the dog were riding in the bed of the pickup. Perkins explained that he was dropped off on the east side of the school at an opening in the fence near the jungle gym, to exercise his dog while his wife and their neighbor proceeded on to the building where his wife's employer had been located.

When he first arrived, Perkins saw three or four kids near the jungle gym, one of whom was about ten years old. Jensen silently decided that the ten year old might have been Mark Prestwood, Justin's friend. Perkins said he began throwing a deflated soccer ball for the dog to fetch in a grassy area just south of the school, and described a couple of children who were playing with a football nearby. Those kids, Jensen believed, had likely been Justin and one of his other friends. At one point Jensen showed Perkins a color photo of Justin and Lee Iseli.

"Do either of these boys look familiar?" asked Jensen. "Do you think that either of these boys were at the playground while you were there?"

Perkins looked carefully at the photo.

"They somehow look familiar," said Perkins. "But I can't place them." He continued to stare at Justin's photo, then said, "Could he have been one of the boys? I'm sorry, but I just can't be sure if either of these boys were on the playground."

Perkins added that he could not remember if there were any children or adults near the volcano area. He said that the park normally got a lot of use, from both children and adults living in the area. Perkins said his wife and neighbor picked him up twenty minutes after having dropped him off. He provided Jensen with a list of his activities and whereabouts from the time he arrived at the school playground until he returned from the Rolling Stones concert in Canada. His wife, neighbor, and others were present

161

when Jensen and Trimble conducted the interview, and each confirmed Perkins's story, providing him with a rock solid alibi. It was obvious to Jensen and Trimble that they had reached another dead end.

The next evening, Friday, November 3, at 7:00 P.M., a candlelight vigil was held for Lee Iseli at Richmond School, where he would have been a kindergartner the following school year. More than three hundred people showed up including friends, neighbors, and investigators. Surveillance was established by FBI Special Agent Michael J. Sanders in an attempt to identify a possible suspect, just in case the killer decided to attend.

Many people cried openly at times during the two-hour vigil, while others held hands and intertwined their arms while singing "Amazing Grace" and "Kumbaya." Hundreds of glowing candles lit up the school playground and served, not only as homage to Lee Iseli, but as a reminder of what can happen to children from any family, anywhere. Some even expressed anger and dismay that their neighborhood had been violated in such an awful manner.

"This isn't about parental judgment," said a neighbor of the Iselis. "It's about a society that

162

tolerates such behavior (from criminals). We want our neighborhoods back."

Sanders and his colleagues contacted a number of individuals at the vigil, and obtained their identification and questioned them. However, they did not consider any of those interrogated a suspect and the surveillance was terminated at 9:00 P.M.

Lee's funeral was held the next day at St. Ignatius Church, located in the neighborhood at 3400 Southeast Forty-third Avenue. Following the Funeral Mass, Lee was buried in the children's final resting area of Mount Calvary Cemetery, located on Skyline Boulevard in the hills above Portland. In a heart-wrenching scene that would last a lifetime, several mourners placed stuffed animals and toys at the grave site, some of which had belonged to Lee.

As on the night before at the candlelight vigil, surveillance was set up at both the church and the cemetery graveside service, to no avail. Although killers have been known to sometimes show up at the funeral services of their victims, Westley Allan Dodd had known better. He knew that the police would be watching and had stayed away.

At 3:20 P.M. that same day, Detective Rick

Buckner conducted a follow-up interview with Patty Griggs,* twenty-five, who had reported seeing a child resembling Lee Iseli with a "bag lady" in the vicinity of Southeast Thirty-ninth Avenue and Hawthorne on the day that Lee disappeared. Buckner visited Patty at her place of employment, a dry cleaning shop, and conducted the interview inside his car.

Patty told Buckner that she had been on her way home from church on Sunday, October 29, at approximately 2:30 P.M., when she noticed a small, blond-haired boy, apparently alone, standing on the southeast corner of the intersection of Southeast Thirty-ninth Avenue and Hawthorne Street. She had been driving southbound on Thirty-ninth at the time, in the outside lane of traffic, and had stopped for a red light. When she looked to her left, she saw the boy standing in front of the Far West Federal Bank building, rubbing his eyes with his right hand. He had appeared to be crying and was looking around, as if searching for someone.

In describing the child, Patty told Buckner that he had bangs that were combed down in the front. He was wearing a light gray jacket with red stripes approximately one-half to three quarters of an inch wide that ran lengthwise from the shoulders down to the wrists on both arms. He was wearing medium blue pants, she thought. Patty watched the child as she waited for the traffic signal to change, and that was when she noticed the bag lady approach him. Patty described the bag lady as between fifty to sixty years old, with graying brown shoulder-length hair. She was wearing either a green hat or a scarf on her head, a dark knee-length jacket, and very dirty white tennis shoes. The bag lady walked up to the child, patted him on the head as if to comfort him, and then turned and walked across the street to her shopping cart which she had left parked by a covered bus stop. Patty didn't think that the child had any connection with the bag lady, but she couldn't be absolutely certain about that because she had been there waiting at the light for such a short time.

At the conclusion of his interview with Patty, Buckner drove around the area that she had described to him and looked for the bag lady. While he didn't consider her a suspect, he hoped that she might have seen something suspicious involving the child and would tell him about it. Buckner briefly recalled details of the bag lady that had already been questioned by one of his colleagues, and although she had said in that interview that she didn't remember a child, Buckner hoped that he could jog her memory on the follow-up. Unfortunately, when

Buckner finally found the bag lady she stuck with her original story and was unable to provide him with any more information than she had related to the original officers who had questioned her. As a result Buckner and the other task force detectives were left wondering whether the boy Patty had seen was really Lee Iseli or some other kid. It would be yet another mystery left unsolved.

And so it went. Report after report about possible sightings of Lee Iseli were called in to the three law enforcement agencies. In a matter of only a few days, police officials estimated that four hundred to five hundred such calls came in, none of which panned out. Not only were they frustrating, but the calls proved time consuming for the investigators because each had to be carefully evaluated and then acted upon or tossed out. After a while the task force detectives felt like they were trapped in a vacuum, insensitive and uncaring, with no way to escape. But things only got worse before they got better.

In the aftermath of Lee's murder, the community reacted in ways that only served to intensify the situation for the police. While people were indeed sorry for the death of the child and for his family, they also became concerned about the safety of their own children like never before. Even though the police hadn't publicly stated it yet, it became very clear to residents of Portland and Vancouver that a child killer was stalking their streets, parks, and playgrounds. Residents didn't need to be told by the police what was going on. All they had to do was open a newspaper or turn on a television.

As public awareness increased, so did reports of attempted child abductions throughout the metropolitan area, many of which were without basis and only served to fuel the fire, so to speak. After a while it became difficult for the police to sort out the actual attempted abductions from those that were merely perceived as attempted abductions. It eventually became so intense that strangers couldn't even look at or say "Hi" to a kid without fear of being reported to the police. Public outrage was soon directed at the law enforcement community as people demanded that the police catch the killer before any more innocent children fell victim to his madness. The police, in a naturally defensive posture, responded that they were doing everything that they could to catch the killer. Frustrated, they eventually began issuing warnings in newspapers, on radio and television for parents to exercise the utmost caution in how they cared for their children. Police stressed that young children should not be left unattended anywhere, and never should they be allowed to walk or play outdoors alone until the killer was caught. In short the two cities were in a panic over the safety of their kids, and virtually all children were incarcerated inside their homes in a parent-imposed jail of sorts while the killer roamed and hunted at will.

As the panic increased, so did the number of hours that the task force detectives were required to work. They were soon putting in eighteen-hour days running down leads and trying to develop new information that they hoped would bring them one step closer to capturing their killer. Detective Dave Rubey was assigned the task of contacting the Oregon and Washington State Corrections Divisions as well as the Psychiatric Security Review Board and the Director of the Community Mental Health Clinics in Portland to request information on possible suspects who might be living in the area. He explained to the director of each organization that they were compiling a list of all known sex offenders in the area deemed capable of killing children, and requested that the information be sent directly to the task force. He was assured that teletypes would be sent as soon as staff from each organization could review their files.

William "Billy" Neer, 10, and his brother Cole, 11, the first victims of Westley Allan Dodd.

Lee Joseph Iseli, 4, Dodd's last known victim.

Entrance to David Douglas Park, Vancouver, Washington, where the bodies of the Neer brothers were found.

Playground of Richmond Elementary School in Portland, Oregon, where Lee Iseli was abducted by Dodd.

Vancouver Lake, where Lee Iseli's nude body was found by a local pheasant hunter.

Lee Iseli's grave site.

New Liberty Theater in Camas, Washington, where Dodd attempted to abduct a six-year-old boy and was apprehended shortly thereafter.

Two police composite sketches of suspects in Neer murders.

Westley Allan Dodd, 28, upon his arrest.

Dodd's Pinto station wagon after police impounded it.

Detective C.W. Jensen, Portland Police Bureau (*left*) and Detective Dave Trimble, Clark County Sheriff's Department.

Detective Randy O'Toole (*left*) and Detective Rick Buckner, Clark County Sheriff's Department.

(*Left to right*), Robert Songer, Clark County Undersheriff; Frank Kanekoa, Clark County Sheriff; and Detective Dave Simpson, Portland Police Bureau at press conference announcing the discovery of Lee Iseli's body.

Dodd's former residence on Northeast 3rd Street, Vancouver, Washington, where he killed Lee Iseli.

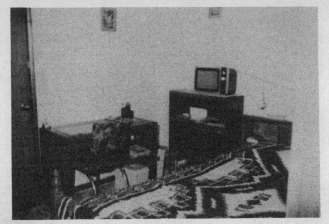

The interior of Dodd's spartan apartment.

Chest of drawers which contained ropes, belts and other restraints.

Dodd's bed as police found it, fitted with ropes to restrain his victims.

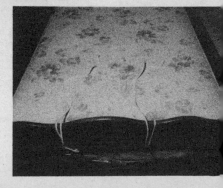

Torture rack, constructed by Dodd himself, upon which the intended to perform "experimental surgery" on his future victims.

The clippings Dodd collected of the Iseli murder.

Briefcase found under Dodd's bed. It contained his album of nude photos of Iseli, taken at various stages of his torture sessions and subsequent hanging inside a closet; Iseli's Ghostbuster underpants; news clippings of his murders; and Dodd's "diary of death".

Copy of the New Testament found in Dodd's apartment in which he scrawled "Satan Lives," "Satan—Love God" and various profanities.

Closet where Dodd hung Lee Iseli's body from a rope around the boy's neck.

Trash barrel where Dodd disposed of Iseli's clothing.

Art Curtis, Clark County Prosecutor, sought the death sentence for Dodd.

Roger Bennett, former Clark County Deputy Prosecutor, worked closely with Curtis on Dodd's prosecution.

Lieutenant Larry Byler, Chief Jailer, Clark County Jail, who—along with other jail officials—witnessed Dodd masturbating in his cell while he recalled details of his crimes.

The exterior of Washington State Penitentiary in Walla Walla on the eve of Dodd's execution.

The author at the outside gate of the penitentiary.

The execution chamber inside the penitentiary in which Dodd's sentence was carried out. (*Courtesy AP/Wide World Photos, Inc.*)

News media satellite trucks in the penitentiary parking lot on the night of execution.

Prison officials prepared the inmate visitation area as a media center for the night of the execution.

Veltry Johnson, Washington State Department of Corrections spokesman, as he briefs reporters concerning the execution procedure and describes Dodd's final hours.

Jerry Davis, the prison's administrative assistant, as he explains the rules of the lottery-style drawing to select the twelve reporters who would witness the hanging.

The reporters selected by lottery to view the hanging as they shared their impressions with the media shortly after the execution.

Darrell Lee, Vancouver attorney appointed to represent Dodd, as he answers questions concerning Dodd's final hours, after the execution.

As a result, the task force soon compiled a list of more than 160 possible suspects with records of sex offenses, each of whom had to be contacted and either eliminated or placed as a higher priority suspect. As the days passed quickly and yielded no results, many of the investigators began to feel that it would take a miracle to solve the case.

In the meantime, Detective Dave Trimble contacted Dr. Ronald Turco, who was not only an M.D. but a sworn police officer with the city of Newberg, Oregon, to see if he could get a better handle on what kind of person would kill a child. After studying a list of qualified professionals in the area, Trimble and the task force had decided that Turco seemed to be among the best qualified from whom to seek information about the elusive child killer.

Turco, Trimble learned, had received a Bachelor of Science degree in chemistry and physics from Pennsylvania State University in the early 1960s, then earned a medical degree from Jefferson Medical College in 1966. He completed his medical/surgical internship at Bryn Mawr Hospital in Bryn Mawr, Pennsylvania, and later studied psychiatry at the University of North Carolina and at the Oregon Health Sciences

169

University in Portland. Turco eventually became director of the Cedar Hills Psychiatric Hospital in Beaverton, Oregon, and began working on criminal cases with the Portland Police Bureau. Over a period of some sixteen years, Turco became involved in hundreds of cases, and did the psychological profile on Randall Woodfield, Oregon's so-called "I-5 Killer." He was part of the investigative team at the Beaverton Police Department which helped lead to Woodfield's arrest and conviction.

After Trimble briefed Dr. Turco on the circumstances surrounding the disappearance and murder of Lee Iseli, Turco, free of charge, discussed the common practices and likely characteristics of the person capable of committing such crimes. A typical offender, said Turco, would be a white male between the ages of twenty-five and thirty-five years. He would be essentially a loner, and would likely have been discharged from the military under less than honorable conditions if he had served. The killer would watch the progress of the investigation closely, and might even try to "assist" the police in an attempt to obtain inside information.

Such a person would also likely keep records of his crimes, including a diary and a file of newspaper clippings covering the crimes. He would likely have a great interest in child pornography, and would probably photograph his victims before and after death. He would drive an older car, and would be employed at a job with limited responsibility, perhaps clerical or even menial labor. The killer would likely have a fetish of some sort, and would almost certainly retain souvenirs or trophies from his victims which he would use while masturbating after the incident to relive the crime.

The offender Turco described would likely prefer male victims because he would view females as "defective." Control over the victims would be the primary motivator for his actions, with sexual gratification being secondary. The suspect would likely have moved around frequently, and probably had murdered before. When arrested, police would likely find the suspect to have a lengthy history of counseling or mental health treatment and a long history of deviant sexual behavior. It would be common for such a person to use restraints on his child victims. Although Trimble and Turco had no way of knowing it yet, Turco had just described Westley Allan Dodd almost to the letter.

In the meantime, while the police seemed to be going in circles, Westley Allan Dodd had al-

171

ready decided how his next victim would die. He would suffocate the next child after tying him down. But he would need something extra to make it more exciting this time, and decided that it was time to construct the torture rack that he had envisioned earlier. Dodd went out to a local lumber store and purchased the wood he would need, then spent his spare time constructing the device. He spent hours measuring, sawing and hammering the wooden pieces together. He completed it by attaching rope restraints at each corner for the victim's hands and feet, and another in the middle to hold his victim's lurching midsection down. When he was finished he stood back and admired his handiwork. Although crude, it would serve its purpose of restraining a helpless, naked boy.

As he began a new fantasy, Dodd took out his diary and started writing an equally new entry dated Thursday, November 9. The next victim, he wrote, "will be tied for a photo as #2 was, then, when finished, he'll be tied just one more time for another picture, but with a bag on his head this time. A *plastic* bag will be put over him and secured about the neck . . . As he suffocates to death, tied down of course. . . ."

Dodd stripped his clothes off and masturbated nonstop until he climaxed. After he cleaned himself off, he drifted in and out of fantasy states for much of the remainder of the night. He repeated the process again the next evening, but altered the fantasy to one of greater intensity:

Incident 3 will die maybe this way: He'll be tied down as Lee was in Incident 2. Instead of placing a bag over his head as I had previously planned, I'll tape his mouth shut with duct tape. Then, when ready, I'll use a clothespin or something to plug his nose. That way I can sit back, take pictures and watch him die instead of concentrating on (using) my hands or the rope tight around his neck — that would also eliminate the rope burns on his neck . . . as Lee had in Incident #2. This is also better than the plastic bag as I can clearly see his face and eyes now . . . as he dies, as well as get some pictures of a naked and dying boy.
Electrocution also a good means for *quick* death.

By Saturday, November 11, Dodd's fantasies were no longer satisfying him. He now needed something more exciting, more stimulating than ever before, and that evening the hunt began anew. Dodd searched through the movie listings in the newspaper until he found a theater where *The Bear* was playing. Shortly after 7:00 P.M. he loaded his "hunting gear" (just in case he needed it) into his yellow 1974 Ford Pinto station wagon and drove to the theater in Vancouver.

At one point Dodd followed a seven- to eight-year-old boy into the bathroom, but quickly decided that he was not as "cute" inside the lighted bathroom as he had been in the dark. But Dodd, now desperate, approached the child anyway.

"You're coming with me," he commanded the boy.

"No," the boy replied, frightened by the demand.

Dodd considered punching the boy in the stomach to knock the wind out of him, but decided that he was too big to carry out of the theater pretending that his "little boy was sick." Sensing that the child might scream or otherwise cause a scene, Dodd decided that he couldn't get him out of the theater quietly and resigned himself to terminate his mission of death.

"Okay, you wait here and I'll leave," said Dodd, who quickly left the theater. He went home and masturbated while fantasizing about what he would have done with the boy if he had gone with him, then watched the news at

11:00 P.M. To his relief nothing was reported about the attempted abduction.

The next evening Dodd went out again. He drove around Vancouver between 5:00 and 7:00 P.M. looking for kids, but found none that he could easily kidnap. As an alternative plan, he drove to the New Liberty Theater in Camas, a small town some fifteen miles east of Vancouver, where *Honey, I Shrunk the Kids* was playing.

He arrived in time for the 9:00 P.M. show, but to his disappointment discovered that there was only one boy there. He was about eight to nine years old, which Dodd considered too old and too large to easily get out of the theater. And besides, he was Oriental, and to Dodd that was a second strike against him. He left for home very disappointed after deciding that the 9:00 P.M. show was too late for the younger kids. He wrote in his diary, "I'll return to the 7:00 P.M. show tomorrow."

Chapter Eleven

Prior to leaving for the New Liberty Theater in Camas, Washington, Westley Allan Dodd updated his diary entries. In an entry dated Monday, November 13, Dodd laid out his future plans and made yet another plea to Satan for assistance:

4:40 P.M. Will now prepare ropes as I had for Incident #2, tied to bed and hidden under it—to use on victims as soon as wanted or needed—needing only to tie loose rope ends to the victim, other ends already attached to bed, or my "rack," my wood framework built for this purpose.

4:45 P.M. I now ask Satan to guide me, and provide or help me obtain a boy tonight. This one I'd like to keep a while—keeping him awake all night each night so he'll sleep all day while I'm at work (tied and mouth taped shut to be on the safe side). I may only keep him two or three days, or even longer if it works out. I'll

176

give him a haircut and buy a new set of clothes for him, to change his appearance in case I take him out as I did Lee in #2. I might even get two boys (perhaps a 6- or 7-year-old taking a 3- or 4-year-old to the toilet?). In the case of two like this — the older (or both) would decide (when I tired of them) which was to die. Don't know if survivor (or just a lone boy) would die, or be used to help get another boy home. Will have to wait and see. I also want to do my medical experiments this time, once finished with sexual play on the body(ies). Also hoping for more, better pictures. May also play "spin-the-bottle" or stripping games, especially with two boys.

5:25 P.M. Now going to Camas — will check out local parks before movie.

Steve Hall,* six, arrived at the New Liberty Theater with his mother, sister, and his mother's boyfriend at approximately 7:30 P.M. for the 8:00 P.M. showing of *Honey, I Shrunk the Kids*. After stopping at the snack bar in the lobby for popcorn, soda pop, and candy, they took their seats in the midsection of the auditorium, about halfway between the screen and the rear of the theater. Dodd, unseen, slipped quietly into the back row, his usual seating preference. Aware that he'd been wrong about the movie's starting time, Dodd was actually grateful because it had caused him to arrive in time for him to see virtually all of the kids who entered the theater.

Fifteen minutes later, Dodd watched a small boy leave the auditorium alone. Not wanting to make the same mistake that he had made at a showing of *The Bear* at the Vancouver Mall Cinemas by waiting too long before following the child, Dodd got up immediately and headed toward the restroom. About that same time Steve Hall told his mother that he had to go to the bathroom. After sliding through a row of crowded seats, Steve walked briskly up the aisle, passed through the double doors that led to the lobby, and entered the restroom. He passed by Dodd, who appeared to the child to be only a harmless-looking, young, dark-haired man, in the foyer that separates the restroom from the lobby.

When Steve entered the restroom, the other small boy that Dodd had followed was using the toilet. Even though Dodd had followed him from the foyer, Steve paid him no mind. After all, Dodd just stood there with a smile on his face and appeared to be a nice man waiting his turn. In fact, he had even motioned for Steve to go on ahead of him when Steve met him in the foyer. When the other boy left, Steve went into the toilet stall. He didn't close the stall door completely because he couldn't see how to latch it, due to the restroom's poor lighting. When he finished, Dodd stopped him as he exited the stall.

"I'm going to take you outside," Dodd told the boy. "I'm not going to hurt you."

"I have to go back and see my mom," responded Steve. "She's waiting for me."

"No, you're gonna come outside with me!"

Without waiting for the boy to say anything, Dodd reached over, picked him up, and hoisted him over his left shoulder. Steve screamed as Dodd walked toward the bathroom door. Dodd, now angry, released his grip enough to enable him to strike the boy with his free hand. Dodd punched Steve in the chest, hard, hoping to knock the air out of him, then tossed him back across his shoulder.

Cathy Asher, thirty-six, one of the theater's co-owners, was standing at the snack bar in the lobby talking to employees Paul Hearn, nineteen, and Amanda Hoffman, eighteen, when she heard the child screaming in the restroom.

"Get in there, Paul, and see what's going on!" said Asher.

As Paul headed into the restroom, he was met

by Dodd, whom he would describe as a small, dark-haired man dressed in a dark ski jacket and blue jeans, who was carrying a small boy in what looked like a bear hug. The boy screamed at the top of his lungs, and kicked violently at the man who was carrying him.

"Calm down, son, calm down," said Dodd as he brushed by Paul in a normal manner through the doors that led to the lobby. At first Paul thought that Dodd was the child's father, as did co-owner Toni Ness, forty-two, who was coming down the stairs from the office when the commotion started. But Steve continued to scream, and Dodd, when he noticed that everyone was watching him, proceeded out the front door with the boy at a fast gait.

"Please help me!" yelled the boy. "Help me! I don't know him! He's trying to hurt me!"

"Come on!" Cathy said to Toni. "We've got to follow him. Amanda, you call 911."

By the time Cathy and Toni reached the outside, they saw the man they would later be able to identify as Dodd running with the boy west down Fourth Avenue and disappearing as he turned the corner onto Birch Street. They followed and, much to their relief, the small blond boy came running down the sidewalk just as they reached the corner. Terrified and crying, he didn't stop until he ran into Toni's legs.

180

"That man's trying to hurt me!" he screamed again as he pointed toward Dodd.

Toni picked the boy up and carried him back inside the theater, where he found his mom and her boyfriend, William "Ray" Graves, thirty-three. When Graves was told what had happened and was given a description of Dodd, he ran out of the theater. He looked up and down the street, but saw no sign of Dodd. He did see Cathy Asher, however, who was talking to a man who identified himself as Bill Hoxsie, twenty. Hoxsie and Cathy were standing beside Hoxsie's pickup truck, which was parked on Birch Street near the theater, talking and looking in the direction that Dodd had fled.

Hoxsie told Graves that he saw the man drop the boy and run to a yellow Pinto station wagon with wood grain sides. The car, he said, had been parallel parked in the first space at the northeast corner of Fourth and Birch. After the man had gotten inside it, he drove off and headed north on Birch. He said that he had watched as the Pinto proceeded in a normal manner, and thought that the suspect had turned west onto Northeast Fifth or Northeast Sixth Avenue. From his vantage point he was sure of the direction, but he couldn't be certain of the street. Hoxsie told Graves that the man was white, five feet seven inches to five feet nine

181

inches tall, approximately 130 pounds with dark hair and a "bony" face. He was wearing dark jeans and a dark jacket. Graves jumped into his own older model car, parked just north of Fourth and Birch, and went after the suspect.

When Graves turned west onto Adams Street and crossed Sixth Avenue, he saw the yellow Pinto just up the street. The car appeared to be lurching, as if the engine was severely misfiring. Graves caught up to Dodd's Pinto near the James River Paper Mill's parking lot on Sixth, not far from the entrance to Highway 14 that leads back to Vancouver. Dodd's car appeared to have stalled, and Dodd was cranking the engine over and over, desperately trying to get it started again. Seeing that Dodd fit the description of the man given to him by Hoxsie, Graves parked his car and cautiously approached the Pinto on the driver's side.

"Looks like you're having car troubles here," said Graves as he spoke to the would-be abductor through the side window. "Doesn't look so good. Want some help?"

Dodd nodded, and Graves told him that he could probably fix the car and get it started for him. He suggested that they push it into the paper mill's parking lot. Dodd didn't object, and apparently viewed Graves's offer as his only chance to get away from the scene of the crime. Along the way Graves continued to ask "innocent" questions until he was satisfied that Dodd was the man who had been inside the theater and was indeed the abductor he was looking for.

After moving the car into the parking lot, Dodd opened the hood and stood looking at the engine with his back to Graves. In the next moment Graves, a heavy construction worker and not someone Dodd would want to reckon with, made his move. He wrapped his right arm around Dodd's neck in a tight choke hold, and seized Dodd's left wrist with his left hand and pulled it behind his back.

"This is it, you sonofabitch!" said Graves. "You've been restrained, and we're going to the cops."

"What's this all about?" asked Dodd.

"Why don't you tell me?" retorted Graves. "Why don't you tell me why you hit the little boy?"

"I haven't hurt anyone."

"Well, then, why were you downtown? Can you tell me that?"

"I went to see the movie."

"Oh, yeah? Well why did you leave before the movie even started?"

"I was just tired, and I was going home,"

protested Dodd.

Graves knew that Dodd was lying, and it pissed him off even more. He wanted to hurt him, but he knew that doing so would be wrong. Instead, Graves kept Dodd in the choke hold and marched him back to the theater where he pinned him against a wall and bound his hands behind him by wrapping his belt around Dodd's slender wrists.

"Good. You caught him," said Toni Ness. Toni and several of the other witnesses told Graves that he had captured the right guy. Instead of questioning Dodd, Graves forced him into a sitting position against a wall in the lobby while they waited for the police to arrive.

A short time later Officer R.L. Strong from the Camas Police Department arrived at the theater. Strong took statements from Ness, Asher, Graves, and several others who had witnessed Dodd as he attempted to take Steve Hall from the theater against his will. After several people positively identified Dodd as the suspect, Strong removed the belt that Graves had used to restrain him and placed him in handcuffs.

"I'll have to place you under arrest and take you in for questioning," Strong told Dodd. He then took Dodd outside, placed him in the back

184

of his cruiser, and drove him a few blocks to police headquarters. After he searched Dodd and placed him in a holding cell, Strong notified Sergeant Don Chaney and Detective Doug Slyter of the attempted kidnapping and subsequent arrest.

When additional help arrived at the police station, Strong and another officer brought Dodd from the holding cell into the booking room for processing. Dodd was given an opportunity to use the telephone, and he called his father.

"I'm in jail," he said. "In Camas . . . tried to take a kid from the theater, I guess." Before ending the call, Dodd asked his father to call his employer, Pac Paper, to inform them that he probably would not be in for work as scheduled for a while.

During the booking process Officer Strong opened Dodd's wallet and found three pieces of identification which showed that he was indeed Westley Allan Dodd.

"Is the wallet and the identification yours?" asked Strong.

"Yes, it is," said Dodd somewhat somberly.

Dodd confirmed that his address was 9816 Northeast Third Street in Vancouver, and told

Strong that he worked as a shipping clerk at Pac-Paper, located at 6416 Northwest Whitney Road, also in Vancouver. Strong logged Dodd's height at five feet nine inches, and weighed him in at 135 pounds. He noted that Dodd's hair was brown and his eyes hazel, and listed as an identifying mark a small scar on Dodd's inside upper left arm. Dodd wasn't asked, and he didn't offer, any other information at that time.

"You're being charged with kidnapping," said Strong. "Do you understand?"

"Yes," replied Dodd, who had been very congenial and cooperative during the booking process. However, as Strong led him back to the holding cell he appeared nervous and his body began to shake somewhat. Strong seized Dodd's jacket, a torn ticket stub, and his shoes, which he entered into evidence. The rest of his belongings, which included thirty-two dollars in currency and sixty-nine cents in coins, a bank card, a Pulsar watch, and his clothes were placed in a locker in the booking facility.

Detective Doug Slyter interviewed the victim, Steve Hall, that same evening. Although Steve was still pretty shaken up over the incident, he took his time and related to the detective all of the details of the attempted abduction and assault against him, and showed Slyter where

Dodd had punched him. Slyter observed a slight reddening of the skin in the area of the boy's sternum, but Steve assured him that he felt okay. As a precaution, Slyter suggested to Steve's mother that the boy should be examined by a doctor.

Following the interview with the boy, Slyter ran Dodd's name and birth date through the National Crime Information Center's (NCIC) computer data banks to pull up his criminal history. Within minutes he knew that Dodd was no stranger to the criminal justice system. His priors consisted of charges of kidnapping, indecent liberties, and lewd and lascivious conduct with a minor under sixteen. Slyter focused on the most recent charge, an attempted abduction in Seattle on June 13, 1987, because it was the charge most consistent with the Camas case involving Steve Hall. He contacted the Seattle Police Department, and a duty officer there agreed to fax the incident report as soon as he could punch it up on the automated records system.

In the meantime Sergeant Chaney arrived at the police station. After Strong and Slyter briefed him on the situation, Chaney sent Officer Brad Conn to the James River Paper Mill parking lot to guard Dodd's car. It was Conn's duty to assure that no one entered or otherwise disturbed the contents of the Pinto. Little did he know that, as the case unfolded, he would be at the site for much of the night.

While reviewing the information they had so far obtained on Dodd, Chaney and Slyter suddenly realized that Dodd's place of employment was located in the Fruit Valley area of Vancouver. What really jumped out at them was the address that Dodd had provided. It was near La Frambois Road and in close proximity to the game preserve and Vancouver Lake where little Lee Iseli's nude body had been found. Furthermore, they noted, Dodd's home address on Northeast Third was less than a mile from David Douglas Park where Billy and Cole Neer were found murdered. After considering the nature of the latest incident involving Steve Hall, the age of the victim, and the fact that Dodd's home and work places were located in areas close to where the three murdered children were found, Chaney decided not to conduct an interview with Dodd until after he contacted the agencies investigating those homicides.

Chaney promptly contacted Detective Sergeant Bob Rayburn and then Detective Dave Trimble at Clark County, and filled them in on the details. Rayburn in turn contacted Detective Rick Buckner, who agreed to go to Camas immediately.

When Buckner arrived he met with Rayburn, Chaney, and Slyter at the police department, and together they drove to the location of Dodd's car. Buckner noted the make and model, and recorded that it bore Washington license plate 288CIU. None of the lawmen entered the vehicle, and instead made their observations from the outside. Using a flashlight and looking in through the rear passenger door window, Buckner could see a charcoal gray piece of material near the edge of the rear seat, which had been folded down. The charcoal gray item was covered with other articles, making it impossible for Buckner to identify it. He noted a pair of brown cloth gloves that were lying on the front console near the driver's seat, and a large tool box in the rear storage area of the car. Since there appeared to be nothing in the car that demanded their immediate attention, such as weapons, they decided to return to the station and wait for Trimble and Jensen to arrive.

Trimble was at home watching Monday night football on television after putting in nearly two weeks of eighteen-hour days when Chaney had called and told him of Dodd's arrest. Jensen also was watching Monday night football when Trimble in turn called him. He, too, was trying to recuperate from the long days of studying the thick file of sex offenders and possible child killers living in the area.

"What do you think, C.W.?" asked Trimble after discussing the situation in Camas with Jensen.

"Well, we have to eliminate him as a suspect or get the background on him," replied Jensen. "Let's roll on in and take care of business now. This can't wait till morning."

Chapter Twelve

It was 10:25 P.M. when Detectives C.W. Jensen and Dave Trimble arrived at the Camas Police Department. There was a distinct autumn chill in the air that night, made all the more apparent because of why they were there. Detectives Jeff Sundby and Darryl Odegard from the Vancouver Police Department were also present, having arrived a few minutes earlier, and they nodded their heads in silent recognition when Jensen and Trimble walked in. After Sergeant Don Chaney briefly outlined the circumstances surrounding Dodd's arrest for everyone, it was mutually decided that Jensen and Trimble would conduct the interview with Dodd because of their familiarity with all of the cases. Dodd was brought out of the holding cell, and official introductions were exchanged at that time.

Prior to the beginning of the interview, Jensen and Trimble provided Dodd with a cup of coffee. Attempting to appear amiable and non-threatening despite the fact that they felt otherwise because of what they now suspected

Dodd of having done, the two detectives escorted Dodd into the Camas Police Chief's office rather than into a cold, austere interrogation room. If they were going to get any useful information out of him, they felt it best that he be made as comfortable as possible while in their presence, and the Chief's office was the most cozy part of the building. The interview officially began at 10:45 P.M. when Trimble read Dodd his Miranda rights from the standard Form 386 Constitutional Rights Warning card. Dodd indicated that he understood his rights, signed the card, and said that he was willing to answer their questions without the presence of an attorney.

To Jensen's and Trimble's surprise, Dodd willingly and openly discussed the incident that had occurred earlier that evening in Camas. He explained to the detectives that he came to the New Liberty Theater because of the children's movie that was playing there, knowing full well that it would bring in a lot of children.

"I thought there might be a bunch of kids there," said Dodd. "So I went in, sat down in the back and started watching the show." He explained that previews of coming attractions and cartoon short subjects preceded the showing of *Honey, I Shrunk the Kids,* and he told of how he saw a young boy leave the auditorium before the movie actually started. Figuring that he was going to a restroom, he followed him. He had just entered the foyer between the restroom and the lobby when a second boy, Steve Hall, entered. Having liked the second boy better than the first, Dodd said that he let him go on in ahead of him.

"I started talkin' to him," said Dodd. "I told him I wanted him to come with me. He said no, started cryin' and hollerin'. I picked him up, got scared and hit him." Dodd told them that it had been his intention to molest the boy right there in the bathroom, but after putting his plan in motion decided that it would be best if he lured the child outside.

The part about his planning to molest the boy in the bathroom was a lie, of course, but Jensen and Trimble had no way of knowing that yet. He had deliberately omitted from the story the fact that he had built a torture rack, especially for his next victim, and the fact that he was going along with them about the Camas incident only because he believed it would get him out of the more serious charges of murder. Dodd hoped that the detectives hadn't connected him to the Neer brothers and Lee Iseli murders yet and that they wouldn't ask him anything about those cases. He kept talking to keep their minds on the Camas case, unaware that they already considered him their top suspect in the murders.

"I left the theater carrying him," he continued. "He was hollerin' and I walked outside and went around the corner, then I let him go. I don't know why, but I let him go. I got to the car, started to drive off, and the car decided to break down on me again. And I got caught. The guy offered to help me with the car and ended up pinnin' me and walked me back to the theater where they kept me until the police arrived."

"How long have you been in Vancouver?" asked Trimble.

"About four months." Dodd explained that he moved into the area four months earlier, in July, after having lived in the Seattle area for approximately three years.

"Where did you live prior to Seattle?"

"I was down in the Tri-Cities for about two years, and I lived in Idaho before that for a couple of years. I moved to Idaho just after I got out of the Navy, which was in '83. Had some trouble in Idaho and some counseling. Couldn't find work. Moved down to the Tri-Cities, that's where I went to high school. I had some friends down there. Started working and my sister and brother-in-law had been trying to get me to move up to Seattle, so I moved up there and got into trouble again."

"What kind of trouble?" asked Trimble.

"I was arrested for investigation of attempted kidnapping. Was finally charged with attempted unlawful detainment, and I got ninety days time served, and one year probation. Got some counseling again, kinda bounced around with the counselors there, and my ex-girlfriend came back to me. I ended up quittin' my job and moved down to Yakima with her. She disappeared a week later and that's when I moved down to Vancouver."

"And that was about four months ago?"

"That's about four months ago, yeah."

"Okay. Where did you move to when you came here?"

"I first moved in with my dad."

"How long did you live there?"

"I was there a little over a month. I had a couple of paychecks to pay rent and the deposit and everything, so I moved right away, over Labor Day weekend. On Labor Day, I was tired from movin' and didn't have a TV or anything, so I started thinkin' about molesting like I done in the past."

Dodd suddenly stopped talking. He realized that he had said too much. He had slipped up, made a critical mistake when he had mentioned Labor Day. If they hadn't been on to him previously, they certainly would be now.

After a short pause, Dodd, with a familiar faraway look in his eyes which meant that he was entering the fantasy land he kept buried in the farther reaches of his mind, began again. He provided the detectives sketchy details of how he had been arrested in the past for a number of sex crimes that began while he was in high school in Richland, Washington, one of the Tri-Cities of Richland, Kennewick, and Pasco. He admitted knowing that he had a serious problem with sexual deviancy and needed psychiatric help. When they pressed him for details, he gave them a more thorough account of "how it all started." His intention, of course, was to set things up like the time he'd been arrested in Seattle so that a lawyer could plea bargain the attempted kidnapping charge down to a lesser offense provided, of course, that they didn't try to bring the murders into it. Dodd knew the system well, as Jensen and Trimble would eventually learn, and he knew how to manipulate it to his advantage.

It all began on July 3, 1970, he said, the weekend of his ninth birthday while his brother and sister were in the hospital having their tonsils removed. He had stopped off at a cousin's house, who had another relative visiting at his house. Both were boys about the same age as Dodd. While the three of them were in his cousin's bedroom, getting ready to go swimming in the cousin's one-foot-deep backyard pool, the two boys told Dodd to watch something. They both pulled down their swimming trunks and touched their penises together. Although Dodd was at first shocked by their actions, he ended up doing the same thing with his cousin.

A few days after that first incident, Dodd recalled having pulled his swimming trunks to his knees and crawled on his arms around his own small swimming pool at home. "Skinny dipping," his relatives had told him it was called. He remembered that he had felt excited about it, but didn't know why.

"So I had, at age nine, had one sexual experience with two nine-year-old boys, and one sexual experience while alone."

Following a bath that same summer, Dodd recalled rubbing some of his mother's hand lotion over *every* part of his body. Although doing this had given him a warm feeling inside, Dodd could not remember if he had an erection while rubbing the lotion into his groin, crotch, and so forth.

"At this point I did not know what it was called," he said. "I'd never heard any of the

197

terms used, such as 'dick,' 'balls,' 'penis,' 'privates,' and so forth."

In an incident toward the end of that summer, Dodd said that he had become upset when asked to change two or three pairs of pants in front of his mother and two or three aunts. They had asked him to show them his new school clothes, and although he had complied he hadn't liked for them to see him in his underwear.

"This gave me a good start on the road to sexual deviancy," he said. "At nine, I was preparing for the fourth grade in Yakima," after having moved from the Tri-Cities. Sometime in May, 1971, with about a month left in the fourth grade, the Dodd family moved again, this time to Umatilla, Oregon.

"I was unhappy at the prospect of moving again," he said. "It had now been three years since I completed one entire school year at one school."

Shortly after his tenth birthday Dodd had his next sexual experience. Again in July, this time it occurred with a neighbor girl Dodd's age who had just moved into the empty house next door to him. After they had become acquainted, the girl asked Dodd and his sister, Kathy, who was four years younger than Dodd, to go into her garage. She said she had something she wanted to show them, something that she had done before.

The girl went to a far corner of the garage, and Dodd and his sister followed. Dodd said his sister was just as interested as he was, though they didn't yet know what was going to happen. The neighbor girl pulled up her shirt a little, then pulled her pants and underpants down to her knees. She remained that way for about five seconds, long enough for Dodd to want to see it again.

"I wanted to study her a little longer—I'd never seen this before. But she said it was my turn," said Dodd.

Dodd said that he pulled his pants down and exposed his penis to the girls. However, he related that he had been disappointed because the neighbor girl wouldn't look at it. Only his sister looked.

"The neighbor girl said that she'd seen it on boys before," said Dodd. "This may explain why a lot of my future victims would be boys."

Dodd said that he couldn't recall any other incidents until the end of his ninth year in school, when he was fourteen. He said that he had been teased and humiliated by girls, and had similar experiences with boys in the locker room. He had become angry by that time, and related how a counselor had told him, following future incidents of exposing and molesting, that he may have simply been trying to "prove" that he was a man. The same counselor had told him that the earlier incidents were just normal childhood experimentation, he said.

In March or April, 1976, Dodd had seen a photograph in an issue of the *National Geographic* that depicted several naked men. He said that the photos had made an impression on him and that he had "snuck" five or six "peeks" at that picture over a couple of days. Even though the photo was not explicit, it had excited Dodd.

The following June, Dodd's parents separated. He said that he had known that it was coming, and their separating had relieved him. He didn't go into detail at this point about *why* the separation had relieved him, but said that it was during that same period that his deviant behavior began.

"Things started out as flashing," he said, "and got progressively worse until I tried to get a boy to go into an empty building with me three days before his eighth birthday. I hoped he would allow me to molest him, perform oral on him and crotch fuck him, but I was prepared for a forced rape. Fortunately, he knew that something was up. I was found innocent of the charge against me, but was offered access to whom I believed is the best counselor in this type of business."

Dodd explained that the junior high school he attended was three blocks from his home, and dismissal was fifteen minutes before the grade school, which was only one block from his home, let out. Dodd's mother and father both worked, and his brother and sister didn't get home until approximately ten to fifteen minutes after the grade school kids walked by their house. Dodd always ran home from school so that he would be there when those kids walked past his house. He would strip off all of his clothes as soon as he entered his bedroom, lubricate his penis and begin masturbating, often in front of them.

"So, at home alone," said Dodd, "I'd yell, 'Hey,' as the younger kids, mostly eight to ten years old, walked by. They'd look up and see me exposing myself from an upstairs window."

Dodd said the flashing occurred eight or nine times over about a three month period. Sometimes he would flash just one boy, and at other times he would flash groups of up to five or six kids, if *most* in the group were boys.

"I never flashed just girls," he said. "Only when they were with a group of good-looking boys between seven and ten years old."

One day Dodd flashed a boy who was walking alone, and the boy simply stared at Dodd as he walked slowly by. Dodd *thought* that the boy had liked it, but that night he found out otherwise. A cop showed up at the Dodd residence and told his mother and father that someone had exposed himself to a boy from their house. Dodd said that even though he had been embarrassed by the disclosure, he had found the flashing experiences to be extremely sexually stimulating.

"Mom and dad wondered if it might have been one of my friends," he said. "But that stopped the flashing, at least from home. School was almost over anyway—there wouldn't be any more kids walking by. . . . I decided to take my flashing on the road. That way, if they told, the police wouldn't know where I lived."

After having decided that it was safer to expose himself to children while away from home, Dodd began riding his bike around town as he looked for victims.

"I'd find a good boy or group of boys, then ride around the block," he explained. "I'd pull my cock and balls out through my fly and hide them by pulling down my T-shirt. Then as I rode by the boys again I'd pull up the shirt and say, 'Hey!'—exposing myself. This happened eight or nine times." Dodd said that he frequently masturbated to fantasies of his behavior.

On one such occasion Dodd encountered three nine year olds and one four year old, all boys, playing. He stopped his bicycle, exposed his penis to them, after which a couple of the older boys yelled, "Do it again!" as he rode away.

"I said, 'I'll do it again if one of you do first,'" said Dodd. "Right there on the sidewalk the four year old pulled down the front of his pants. He only exposed his groin, but wouldn't do it again. They all said, 'Now you again.'

"I took them into their yard behind some shrubs and pulled down the front of my shorts," Dodd continued. "I wore no underwear on these trips. I said, 'Anyone want to touch it?' The four year old did and said, 'Yep—it's real!' They all laughed, and the four year old and two of the nine year olds agreed to meet me at a vacant field nearby that evening so I could do it again and show them some tricks such as making it 'bigger,' 'bouncing' it without touching it, and making 'stuff' come out. I told them I might even teach them how to do it, but they never showed up. . . . That was the last time I ever just flashed a kid. One had touched me, and that had given me a better feeling than just showing myself. I now wanted be touched, not seen."

Jensen and Trimble occasionally glanced at each other and threw out a question, but they were careful not to reveal their disgust and disdain for the pervert who sat in front of them revealing his life of sordid activities. At times it seemed like he was actually enjoying relating his random experiences to them, and he would frequently get that faraway look in his eyes, as if entering a fantasy state even as he spoke. They let him go on.

His problem, he said, had now become one of getting a child to actually touch him without scaring him off. By that time he and his family had moved back to the Tri-Cities. He soon found the solution to this problem when he stumbled upon a group of six kids, three boys and three girls, in a school playground. His desire to be touched had become so intense that he no longer worried too much about the location, the number of children present, or even whether they were boys or girls. If they were

204

kids, they would do.

"I asked the kids if they wanted to play a game, and they did," he said. "They asked, 'What?' I told them to line up their backs to me and that I'd put something into their hands, one by one, and they'd have to guess what it was without looking. I gave them a rock, then an ink pen. Then I said, 'I'll have to hold the next one so it doesn't get broke.' I reminded them not to look, and let each one wrap their hand around my cock for two or three seconds.

"None of them knew what it was when I asked them," he continued. "But one boy said he might know, that he'd try again. They each tried again, but still didn't know what it was. Afterward, I pointed to my now-covered parts and said, 'This.' The one boy said, 'Yeah—I knew it!' I asked him if he'd go to a more private area and do it again, and he said he would if everyone else went. But the rest didn't agree."

Approximately two weeks later, unable to find any boys that he could approach, Dodd said he found and settled on three girls. They were at a playground and all of them were sitting on swings. One of them, about six or seven, was topless, and he spotted her shirt lying on the ground. He went up to the topless girl first.

"Are you a boy or girl?" he said he asked. "She said, 'A girl.' One of the other two girls, who were eight or nine, said, 'He just wants to see your kee-kaw.' "

Upon being asked, the three girls played the same guessing game with Dodd as had the previous kids. When he asked them if they wanted to see "it," they said "yes."

"I said," continued Dodd, " 'I will if one of you will.' All three girls agreed that the youngest one would drop her pants. But she got scared and started to run. I chased and caught her. She fell to the ground on her back. I got down on my knees, straddled her legs and started to unsnap her pants. She started crying, so I let her go."

A school janitor apparently had seen what Dodd had done with the girls, including the "game," and approached Dodd afterward. He asked him if he wanted to come inside for a while. Dodd, thinking that he was going to call the police on him, refused. Dodd said that he learned, a few months later, that a janitor at the school had been fired for raping a seven-year-old girl and an eight-year-old boy.

"He almost had a fifteen-year-old boy—me!" said Dodd.

A few days later the youngest girl from the school playground incident showed up on

Dodd's doorstep with her father. After disclosing the incident to Dodd's father who, according to Dodd, beat him for the episode, he decided to give up on trying to get strangers to touch him sexually.

By then Dodd said that it no longer mattered to him whether he molested boys or girls. Even though he was fifteen, he still hadn't been taught about having sex. As far as he was concerned, touching was what sex entailed.

One day, however, still in 1976, some of Dodd's cousins came over to his house. Among them was a nine-year-old girl, and he played his guessing game with her. He said that she knew that it was his penis that he had placed in her hand, but at his suggestion agreed to go into a closet with him for another guessing game.

"In the closet I had her hold my dick for a few seconds," he said as he recounted the episode. "Then I had her pull on it as hard as she could. I had her feel my balls. Then I had an idea! *I* could touch a kid, instead of just kids touching me!"

Dodd said she agreed to pull her pants down as long as he left the closet door closed so that he couldn't see her, and that had made him happy. He placed his hands on her hips and could see her outline in the darkness.

"I asked if I could 'touch it.' She said, 'Oh God,' which was her favorite expression. I put my lips against her 'kee-kaw,' which was the only name I knew it by, thanks to the girls at the school, and I blew on it.' A few days later, when we were at her house, she told my sister and her eight-year-old brother what we'd done, but they didn't believe her. I said, 'Let's do it again.' She said, 'Where?'

" 'Right here, so we can show them so they'll believe us,' " Dodd recounted. "She pulled down her pants. I said, 'Lay on the end of the bed.' She did, pants around her ankles, legs bent at the knees over the end of the bed. I helped her spread her legs out and got my first *good, close* look at a girl.

"I saw that she didn't wipe very good," he continued. "There was a crusty film around her 'kee-kaw.' I almost didn't do it, but decided it was that way when I did it in the dark closet, too. My sister and her brother watched as I again blew out against her 'privates.' She then helped me talk her brother into trying it. This was the first time that I had an eight-year-old cock in my mouth. I just blew it right back out. Later, alone with her brother, I put a hand down the front of his pants as I leaned over his

208

shoulder from behind. I wanted to know what he felt like. He made me stop by saying he'd 'tell.' I stopped."

Dodd explained that he was soon questioned about other incidents that had occurred around town involving flashing and asking kids to pull down their pants. A clarinet player in his high school band, he was forced to miss a band trip at the beginning of his sophomore year because of the investigation. He said that he hadn't exposed himself or committed any other molestations until approximately January, 1977, because of his brush with the law. Despite the investigation no charges were filed because the police considered Dodd a "nice kid," and because he had agreed to go to therapy. Dodd said that he went to the counseling sessions for about two months, then quit.

Dodd told the detectives that he worked as a stock boy at a grocery store for two years after graduating from Columbia High School in Richland in 1979. Two years later he joined the U.S. Navy, in part to avoid having charges filed against him for more molestation incidents. He spent two years in the Navy, but was given a "General Discharge" for disciplinary reasons. When asked to explain, he said that the discharge was the result of an incident in which he had approached two young boys and had attempted to entice them into going with him by offering them money. After he had molested them, they reported the incident, and he was arrested within a few days by the Military Police.

Following his discharge from the Navy, Dodd moved to Lewiston, Idaho, where his father was living at that time. While in Idaho he engaged in multiple sexual encounters with two boys who were friends of his family. He said that he had frequent contact with one of the boys, during which he performed oral sex on him. Dodd said that he was eventually arrested, convicted, and did some actual jail time. However, his sentence was soon commuted to probation, a condition of which required him to attend counseling on a regular basis.

Dodd said that he hadn't objected to continuing with the counseling until he was required to attend group therapy sessions. As soon as his probation ended, he stopped attending the sessions because he found that he could not talk about his problems in front of a group of people.

"Do you feel sorry for the molestations and sexual contact you've had with kids in the

210

past?" Trimble asked at one point.

"Yes, I do."

"What do you think would help you to change your behavior?"

"I need therapy, more counseling."

"Do you feel that you might continue to hurt children if you do not receive therapy?" Trimble seemed to be setting him up, perhaps for a future question.

"Yeah, I believe that I would." Dodd, his guard now down, added that his sexual encounters had become more intense with each subsequent incident, and as a result were becoming more serious.

"Are you aware of the recent homicides in the Vancouver area involving young boys?" Trimble threw out the question without warning. From the look on Dodd's face, the question had caught Dodd off guard, just as Trimble had wanted.

"Yes. I've read about them in the newspapers." Dodd, attempting to remain calm, said that he had seen composite drawings of possible suspects in those slayings and had become concerned about them because the composites somewhat resembled himself. He insisted, however, that he was not involved in either the Neer case or the Iseli case.

Dodd would later tell this writer that he had

decided early on that he would deny being involved in the murders if questioned about them. His game plan had been to get the cops to focus on the attempted kidnapping and his past sex crimes, and to steer them away from the murders.

"There are numerous circumstances, Wes, which can implicate you as a likely suspect in these homicides," said Jensen. "There had been no recent child killings in this area until shortly after you moved here." Jensen pointed out as another example the close proximity of Dodd's employer to the area where Lee Iseli's body was found near Vancouver Lake. That, said Jensen, coupled with the fact that Dodd lived close to the park where the Neer brothers were murdered and the fact that his preference for sexual encounters with young boys was unmistakable tended to implicate him in the murders.

"Oh, my God!" said Dodd. "I like kids. I love little children. I would never hurt a child." Dodd's hands were now trembling, and his voice had a slightly discernible quaver to it.

Jensen, sensing that Dodd wasn't being truthful, continued to push him. He asked Dodd if he could recall what he was doing on Sunday, October 29, the day Lee Iseli was kidnapped in

212

Portland. Dodd said that since it was a Sunday he probably did not work that day but likely spent the day alone watching football on television. However, he was unable to provide Jensen and Trimble with the name of any person who could corroborate his story or provide an alibi for him.

"I know I wasn't in Portland that day," said Dodd. "I never go to Portland." He explained that he never went very far from home because of car problems.

"Look, you can't blame us for asking," said Jensen.

"No, I don't."

"Look, Wes, we have to clear you out of this," said Jensen. "We have to prove one way or the other if you're involved. If you were me, what would you do?"

"I guess I'd talk to people who knew me."

"What else?"

"I don't know."

"How about searching your car and house?" suggested Jensen. "Detective Trimble and I would have to do that. You can make it easy by giving us your consent to search."

"I'd have to think about that," said Dodd. "Talk to an attorney."

"Do you have a problem talking to us?" asked Jensen. "Do you want an attorney present while

213

you talk to us?"

"No," said Dodd.

"Something's bugging you," tried Jensen. "It's obvious that there's something you possess that will implicate you in these crimes. Otherwise, you'd give us a consent to search. We're here to help you, Wes. You've got something hurting you inside."

At that point Dodd sighed deeply and leaned forward in his chair. He bowed his head, and tears began to form in his eyes. He looked as if he was ready to cry.

"May I have some water?" asked Dodd.

"Sure," said Trimble. "I'll get you some." Trimble left the room briefly, and when he returned he handed Dodd a cup of water.

After some hesitation, Dodd told the detectives that they would find a certain key on his key ring. The key, he said, would unlock a briefcase that they would find beneath his bed. Inside the briefcase, he said, they would find photos of Lee Iseli and other items that pertained to the murders of the Neer brothers. Jensen and Trimble looked at each other without expression, each realizing they would be up for many hours. Not only would they have to obtain a more complete statement from Dodd, the two detectives also knew that they had a lot of leg work to complete in the upcoming days. Sleep, they knew, had suddenly become a luxury.

"Okay, Wes," said Jensen. "Let's go back to the beginning."

Chapter Thirteen

At approximately 11:10 P.M. that same day, while Jensen and Trimble continued their interview with Dodd at the Camas Police Department, Camas Police Detective Doug Slyter and Clark County Sheriff's Detective Rick Buckner arrived at the Northeast Vancouver home of Westley James Dodd, also known as Jim Dodd, Westley Allan Dodd's father. Upon arriving at the residence, the detectives noticed that there were no lights on inside the house and there were no cars parked in the driveway. It appeared to them that everyone was in bed.

Undaunted by the prospect of awakening someone at that hour, especially since he had been informed that Dodd had called his father from the Camas Police Department earlier that evening to tell him about his arrest, Buckner knocked on the front door and rang the door-bell for approximately two minutes. Finally a sleepy-eyed man approximately fifty years old came to the door. The two detectives identified themselves and apologized for having to be there at such a late hour and for waking him up, and the man in turn identified himself as Mr. Dodd. When asked if they could speak with him, Dodd invited them inside. They were joined a few minutes later in the living room by a woman who explained that she was Westley Allan Dodd's stepmother. Slyter explained the circumstances surrounding Westley's arrest that evening in Camas as Jim Dodd and his wife listened intently.

"It all started in the Tri-Cities," said Dodd in a somewhat dejected tone. He explained that Westley, his oldest son, had been arrested by the Richland Police Department while he was still in high school, but was not certain of the precise details. Westley, he said, had been living with his mother at the time. Dodd also mentioned the fact that Westley had been discharged from the Navy while stationed in Bremerton after apparently attempting to lure some young kids away from a gymnasium and follow him.

"Wes has been treated by a private counselor and has gone to other treatment programs, but nothing really seemed to help him," said Dodd. He then told how his son had been arrested in Lewiston, Idaho, in 1983 or 1984, after having lived with a woman who had three kids. The two detectives knew that such behavior was consistent with pedophiles in general, who were known to seek out and form relationships with single women with children for the sole purpose of molesting the kids.

"Did the arrest in Lewiston have anything to do with child abuse or sexual abuse of the children?" asked Buckner.

"I don't know," said Dodd, explaining that since he and Westley's mother divorced he was not always aware of all of the details surrounding his son's brushes with the law. He said that Westley moved from Renton, Washington, and in with them on July 27, 1989, and they had gone camping together on the Olympic Peninsula until the first week in August.

"Does Westley have any family, relatives, or friends in the Portland area that he might visit?" asked Slyter. Unknown to Dodd, Slyter was fishing, trying to establish a connection between Dodd's son and Portland.

"Not to my knowledge," replied Dodd. He said that he and Westley's mother, Carol, divorced in 1977, and that she moved to Minnesota a few years later.

"When was the last time that Westley saw his mother?" asked Slyter.

"I don't think Wes has seen her since she went back to Minnesota," said Dodd. "That was about four or five years ago."

"Has Westley ever been arrested in the Portland/Vancouver area?" asked Buckner.

"No, not to my knowledge."

When asked to characterize Westley for them, Dodd told the detectives that he considered his son to be a very passive type and a music lover. He said that Westley had never been married, and when he had stayed with him and his stepmother Westley would go to work during the day and then come right home. He did not go out much at night. Dodd described his son as a loner, someone who did not make friends easily despite the fact that he had no problem when it came to talking to people. Dodd told the detectives that Westley would probably "talk your ears off" if given a chance. Dodd also mentioned that Westley never brought any friends home, and he didn't know of any friends that he might have had.

"Would you consider Westley an organized or disorganized type of person?" asked Buckner.

"A little bit of both," said Dodd.

Sometimes Westley would be extremely organized if it pertained to something he was really interested in or cared about, said Dodd. At other times he seemed very disorganized. When asked whether Westley had ever been molested when he was young, Dodd responded that he did not know if he had been or not. Slyter and Buckner thanked the Dodds for their help, but made no mention at that time that their son was being looked at as a suspect in the Neer brothers and Lee Iseli homicide investigations.

Upon their return to the Camas Police Department, Buckner and Slyter conferred with the other investigators regarding their meeting with Dodd's father and stepmother. They also discussed what to do with Dodd's car, and it was finally decided that it would be photographed at the parking lot where it was still parked and then moved. After Buckner took a number of photos, he sealed the doors and windows with evidence tape to ensure that nobody entered the vehicle undetected, and then called a local towing company which removed the car to a secure location. It would be processed for clues later.

Meanwhile, Jensen and Trimble continued their interview with Dodd. After they had asked him to go back to the beginning and because he began talking about the murders of Billy and Cole Neer, Jensen and Trimble asked that Vancouver Detective Jeff Sundby be present. When Sundby took a seat across from him, Dodd explained how he had found the two boys at David Douglas Park on Labor Day.

"I knew where David Douglas Park was," said Dodd, "and thought it might be a place where I could find a boy and get him alone. I'd been in the park about an hour and a half, maybe a little longer, and was walkin' down through woody trails when I found them near the center of one of the trails. They had their bikes with them."

"Did you have any weapons at that time?" asked Trimble.

"I had a knife, a fish-fillet knife underneath my right pant leg," said Dodd.

"This fish-fillet knife; can you tell me what that looks like?," asked Sundby. "There's all kinds of those on the market."

"It had a light brown handle. It was a six-inch fillet knife, had a six-inch blade. It was a long blade, a narrow skinny one," said Dodd.

The detectives also knew just how sharp and deadly fish-fillet knives were. They had seen pictures of how other victims, not connected to this investigation, had been literally disemboweled with such a knife, and knew what type of damage it was capable of doing in the hands of someone who wanted to get messy. They asked Dodd to continue, to tell them what happened after he encountered Billy and Cole.

"I walked up to 'em and said, 'I want you two to come with me.' I made them follow me down toward the end of the park, off towards Andresen, and took the boys into the wooded area up off the trail. Told 'em I wanted one of 'em to pull their pants down. I said I wouldn't let 'em go 'til one of 'em did. By then I'd been asking questions and knew Billy was ten and Cole was eleven. I said, 'One of you pull your pants down.' Billy said 'him' and pointed to his brother. Cole asked me 'why' and I said because I told you to. So he did. . . .

"I kept tellin' 'em everything's gonna be okay, that I wasn't gonna hurt 'em. Cole pulled down his pants. I did oral sex on him for a little bit, an' then I let him pull his pants back up and turned to Billy and said, 'Okay, now I want you to pull yours down,' but he said 'no' and started to cry. So I told Cole to pull his down again, which he did, and I had him turn so his back was towards me. I undid the front of my pants and pulled out my penis. I had intended to put my penis between his legs to simulate intercourse and, ah, I couldn't get an erection so I gave up on that, refastened my pants and told the boys, 'Okay, there's one more thing.' I pulled the knife out from under my pant leg.

"Billy was off to my right, 'bout a foot off of me diagonally," Dodd continued. "Cole was off on my left. And I reached over and stabbed Billy with the knife. Then I turned to Cole and stabbed him two or three times. While I was stabbing Cole, Billy got up and started to run.

He ran back down the hill to the trail, and just started runnin' up the trail towards Andresen. I ran after him and caught him, spun him around and I stabbed him, I don't know, two, three more times, and he ran back in the direction of the park again."

"So you ran back into the park?" asked Sundby.

"I was running back up through the trails and I had my car up in the parking lot by the ball fields. I stopped, decided I'd better go back to where I had the two boys together and make sure I didn't drop anything, leave anything behind that might identify me. Went back up, had a little trouble finding the spot, then I saw Cole laying there and I knew he was dead. His eyes were open, his head was to the side and he wasn't movin' at all. It almost made me sick. I thought, well I really cut him up pretty bad. I thought his intestines or somethin' was hangin' out, then I realized that he never had a chance to pull his pants back up. At least that's what I think happened, but I didn't really look that close. I was more interested in making sure I hadn't lost anything more . . . there were a lot of people that saw me there."

"Where was the knife at when you ran out of the park?" asked Trimble.

"When I was running I was carrying the knife

223

in my hand," said Dodd. "When I started walking, before I walked up the trail back into the main part of the park, then I put it back underneath my pant leg . . . into a sheath I had for it. I noticed there didn't seem to be too much blood on the knife, and I thought about just leaving it there. Then I figured, no, there'd be fingerprints. When I got home I wrapped it up in a bunch of paper and ended up throwin' it away."

"Do you remember where you threw it?" asked Sundby.

"In a big garbage bin at work. I ended up taking the knife to work with me on the Wednesday morning after the incident and dumped it in the garbage Dumpster out there. The Dumpster gets dumped anywhere from two to five times a week, and I knew nobody'd find the knife there."

"Why did you feel that you needed to kill the boys?" asked Trimble.

"So they wouldn't tell, wouldn't be able to identify me," said Dodd. "When Cole pulled his pants down, I knew I wouldn't be able to let them go."

"Did you keep anything that they had with them?" asked Trimble.

"No."

"Nothing at all?"

"No."

"Did you keep the newspaper articles about the murders?" asked Trimble.

"I kept all newspaper articles that I found about it."

"Where are they now?"

"They're in that briefcase in my apartment."

"Do you remember what you were wearing that day?" asked Trimble.

"I had on blue jeans, had a T-shirt I think, I don't remember for sure."

"Do you ever wear a hat?" asked Jensen.

"I did have a hat on," said Dodd.

"Do you remember what kind?" asked Jensen.

"I've got two hats. They're both blue hats. One says, 'Don't worry, be happy' on the front. The other one, I don't remember what it says. They've both got some white and red lettering on them."

"What about Lee Iseli?" asked Jensen.

After a short pause, as if he was pulling his thoughts together, Dodd described in intricate detail how he had come across Lee Iseli at the Richmond School playground and coaxed him into leaving with him. He said that he used a lot of baby talk with Lee, and that seemed to work best.

"When we got home, I told him to take off his clothes," said Dodd. "At first he said 'no.' And then I said, 'yeah, you have to.' I wasn't talking angry with him or anything. I was trying to keep him calm. And when I said, 'well, you have to,' I pulled off one of his shoes. At that time he started taking off his shirts and I finished taking off his other shoe and socks. I put all of his clothes aside and had him lay on the bed. I've got a Polaroid camera and I took some pictures of him."

"Where are those pictures now?" asked Trimble.

"Uh, they're in the briefcase in my apartment."

"What was Lee wearing that day?" asked Trimble.

"He had been wearing blue pants, um, a white T-shirt that had some writing of some kind on the front. He had brown, almost moccasin-like shoes, a sweatshirt that zipped part way down the front — gray and red I think. Um, had him on the bed, took some pictures of him, and told him, 'Now I'm gonna teach you how adults make love.' I kissed him a few times and had him kiss me back. Um, after I took the pictures of him, I had taken my clothes off, too. I let him get underneath the covers in bed and I got in underneath with him. And that's when I kissed him. Well, then, I had him roll over on his stomach and I pushed the covers back off the bed and put my penis between his legs and started simulating intercourse with him. I had him roll over onto his back and kept on with the intercourse that way. When I was done, I cleaned him up, I cleaned myself up, and let him get dressed again."

"When you said you cleaned up, does that mean you ejaculated on him?" asked Jensen, feeling nauseous.

"Yeah, I ejaculated on him and I cleaned him up. In fact, I told him beforehand that in a little bit, some white stuff was going to come out and I was going to let it come out on him."

"Did you ever have to restrain him in any way to keep him from moving about?" asked Jensen.

"No. Right after I got him home, I tied him down just to get pictures of him, of him being tied up and then I untied him right away."

"Explain that to me." Jensen couldn't understand why Lee had ligature marks on his ankles and wrists if Dodd had let him go right away, but he didn't tell Dodd what he knew.

"I had ropes tied to the corners of the bed, and I tied these around his ankles and wrists and I took a picture of that and then I let him go right away. I had told him that I was going to do that beforehand." Dodd apparently wasn't going to explain the ligature marks, but it didn't take a particularly vivid imagination to visualize what had likely occurred while Lee had been tied down.

"What kind of rope did you use to restrain him?" asked Trimble.

"It was just a small cotton rope that I used, kind of like the type you make a clothesline out of. It was a pretty small diameter, made out of cotton." He then explained how he had taken Lee out to Kmart and to McDonald's that evening.

"Did Lee ever ask you to take him home?" asked Trimble.

"There was one time that he said, 'I want to go home now,'" said Dodd. "It was after we had been to McDonald's and we had gone back to my apartment. And I said, 'Aren't you having fun? I thought you were going to spend the night with me.' And he said, 'Oh, yeah,' and forgot about wanting to go home. Instead, he wanted to stay up all night.

"I poured myself a cup of coffee and set it on the desk, where Lee was drawing pictures. He knocked the cup over and spilled the coffee on himself. It was real hot coffee and he started grabbing his shirt and I told him to take it off. I helped him get his sweatshirt off and noticed that his chest was red. It did burn him a little bit, so I got a cold, damp rag to put on his chest and had him lay on the bed."

Dodd said that he gave Lee one of his own T-shirts to wear until Lee's dried out. While Dodd watched television, Lee continued to draw pictures.

"He was wanting to stay up all night," said Dodd. "He said that he did that at home sometimes. He talked for awhile, said that his mom had gone away. When I asked him if he lived with his mom or dad, he started talking about the mail lady and how nice she was. Finally, at about ten or ten-thirty, I told him that it was time for bed. He kept arguing that he wasn't ready for bed, that he didn't have any pajamas to wear. I pointed out that he had my T-shirt on and that it went all the way down to his knees, and said that he could just use it for his pajamas.

"I asked him if he wanted to sleep in the bed with me or if he'd like me to get a sleeping bag out for him. And he said, 'No, that's okay,' he'd sleep in the bed with me. I'd have probably made him sleep in the bed anyway."

Dodd, again in intimate detail, described how he molested Lee Iseli throughout the night, stopping only to nap briefly. He ended with his summation of the murder.

"About five-thirty in the morning, it was getting close to time for me to have to get up and get ready to go to work, Lee was on his back sound asleep. I moved him towards the center of the bed a little bit, he had his legs together. I was lying on my left side facing him and his right arm was pinned between his body and mine. I put my right leg up over his legs to hold him down, I put my left hand up around his head and held his left hand down and with my right hand I started choking him. I started getting tired, and he was still struggling a little bit. He got his legs free and was trying to use his legs to push away from me. My right hand was getting tired so I started using both hands to choke him. He finally quit struggling and I let go. I decided to see if that CPR stuff really worked, so I blew into his mouth once. I decided, 'nah, no sense doing that.' "

As Dodd spoke, the detectives noted, he displayed a mild sense of fear but showed a greater sense of pleasure while relating all of his actions. It was repugnant and loathsome to the detectives, but they tried hard not to let their feelings show. Now that he had gone this far, they wanted Dodd to keep talking.

"Anyway," Dodd continued, "he'd lay on the bed and he started breathing again. I had thought that he was dead, but he wasn't. He was having some trouble breathing, but he

230

started breathing. So I took a piece of that rope and wrapped it around his neck a couple of times and pulled it tight. Holding the rope, I pulled him up onto my lap to keep him upright. I kept choking him with the rope. His chest, uh, was still heaving a little bit. I figured I'd probably been trying to choke him for two minutes or so already. I didn't know how much longer it was going to take so, using the rope, I carried him over to the closet and tied the end of the rope around the clothes rack. I left him hanging there, and I took a picture of it. I went and used the bathroom, and about ten minutes later came back and cut him down. I set his body up on the shelf in my closet."

"In what position?" asked Trimble.

"In kind of a sitting position," said Dodd. "He had his knees up to his chest. He was in a small area of the closet, a real narrow closet, and he was kind of leaning over against the side and back walls." Dodd explained how he had concealed Lee's body with a sleeping bag, blankets, and a pillow.

"I got ready for and went to work," Dodd continued. He said that the only thought he had during the day at work was returning home so that he could have anal sex with Lee Iseli's body. "I got home probably a little bit after four that afternoon. Took his body down out of

231

the closet and noticed that he was real stiff and cold and, um, purple. Um, laid him on the bed, took a couple of pictures, loosened up his legs so that I could lay him down on his stomach. And then I put on a condom and had anal sex with him, with his body. Afterward I cleaned up, took a shower.

"It must have been about seven or so when I put his body in a couple of garbage bags and carried him out to the car. I'd never been out to Vancouver Lake, but I drive past a sign every day on the way to work that says public fishing and I knew the lake was there. I drove out there, found the sign, drove out the road. It was dark and I realized it was a dead-end road. Pulled over, took him out of the car. It was dark, so I left the headlights on so that I could see where I was going. Walked out into the brush a few feet, dumped his body out of the bags, got back in the car and left."

"Were there any other cars down there?" asked Trimble.

"No, I didn't see anyone else down there at all," said Dodd.

"Were these garbage bags new ones, or had they had stuff in them before?" asked Jensen.

"They were brand-new ones." Dodd explained how he had gone out briefly and bought them, along with a package of condoms.

"What condition was Lee's body in when you left it?"

"He was face up, um, purple, his arms were still stiff. I had loosened up his legs a little earlier."

"What was he wearing?" asked Trimble.

"Nothing. He hadn't worn anything since I pulled his pants off right after he went to sleep."

"What did you do with his clothes?"

"My landlady has a burning barrel out behind the house and I put a box of newspapers in it and burned the clothes. I kept his underwear."

"Why did you keep his underwear?"

"For masturbating."

"Where is it now?"

"It's in my briefcase."

"What did you do with the rope?"

"I burned that too."

"Did you keep the newspaper articles about Lee's disappearance?"

"Yeah."

"Where are they?"

"They're in the briefcase also."

"Did you keep a diary of your activities?"

"Yes, I did." Dodd said the diary outlined the murders, and included times, locations, what he did to his victims, and so forth.

"Where is it now?"

"In the briefcase with everything else."

At one point the fax of an incident report involving Dodd came in from the Seattle Police Department. It was several pages long, and was listed as case number 87-290624, written up by Officer C. Farrell. The detectives passed it around to each other.

When Jensen, Trimble, and Sundby presented the prior criminal history to Dodd, he made no attempt to deny it. He explained that he had moved in with his sister and her husband in nearby Renton, where they were managing a small apartment complex just north of Seattle. After obtaining a job as a security guard, Dodd said that he was stationed at a construction site at night and on weekends. He said the incident had occurred on the morning of June 13, 1987.

"There was a motel next door to the construction site," said Dodd. "It had weekly and monthly rates, and there were a lot of kids living there. One little boy, I believe he was about seven . . . wandered to the construction site. I was walking around on one end of the building at the far end of the site and I saw him fall. It looked like he had hurt himself because he stayed down on the ground. I ran up to him, helped him get back on his feet and made sure

234

he was okay. The next day he came back and thanked me for helping him and wanted to know if there was anything he could do for me. I told him, 'No, there wasn't anything that I needed.'

"The next day I was off duty, but I went back up to the site knowing that he would be there. I had intentions of getting him into one of the vacant buildings and molesting him . . . I was going to take the boy out into the woods, several miles away, rape him, and then I was going to kill him. . . ."

Dodd said that he had already picked out the place where he was going to kill him, and that the incident had been the first in which he had planned to kill a kid.

"But the kid was smart. He knew that something was wrong, and used his story of going to get toys for the boy that I was supposedly looking for to get away."

Dodd said that he was initially charged with attempted kidnapping, but following a nonjury trial his lawyer plea bargained the charges down to attempted unlawful detainment. It had taken three months, during which time Dodd had spent in jail, but the judge credited him for time served and placed him on a year's probation. Because of Dodd's prior background of exposing himself and molesting children, the judge ordered that he receive outpatient counseling, which he said he quit as soon as his probation was completed.

"At that time a friend of mine and his girlfriend's daughter came up, and me and the daughter kind of fell in love," said Dodd, explaining what happened in his life after the Seattle incident. "She disappeared on me about a month and a half later, but came back a few months ago after being gone more than a year."

Dodd said that the woman explained to him that she had been pregnant with his son when she left, and that had been the reason for her leaving. She brought the baby with her, but Dodd said that he wasn't one hundred percent certain that he was the father. He felt pretty certain that he was the boy's father, but not absolutely certain. There was room for doubt, he said.

"So I quit my job and we moved down to Yakima to be with all of her friends and family," said Dodd. "We were there for about a week when she disappeared on me again. She just took off, and left me with nothing. I had to sell everything I had at the time, which was very little, just to get enough gas money to get down to Vancouver where my dad was living. And that was about four months ago."

"Okay," said Trimble. "Did you know what

you were doing was wrong?" He was trying to bring Dodd back to the subject of the murders, and to determine if there was premeditation and intent on Dodd's part.

"Yeah. I knew it was wrong." Dodd explained that his sexual fantasies had progressed to the point where he no longer was excited by the sex, but by the violence of his acts.

"I mean what made you know it was wrong?"

"Doing something like that to a kid, I just knew that it was wrong," said Dodd. "Um, you hear about it on the news, TV, and everything all the time. I knew that it was wrong. And it would stop me for a while. But after a while things started building up again, stress, things on the job, things just not going good. And after a point, I couldn't really control myself any longer."

"Would you have done these things if some-one had been there to watch what was going on?"

"Nope."

"What kinds of things did you do to avoid being caught?"

"I would try and make sure I was in areas where there was no one else around, like I did with the Neer boys at David Douglas Park. And with Lee, I didn't see any other adults around at all, so I walked up and talked to him."

237

"You said earlier, in both cases, that you destroyed some evidence or got rid of what was used. Was that to avoid getting caught?" asked Trimble.

"Yeah, that was in case anything happened, there wouldn't be any evidence."

"What did you do to resist the impulse to do this on other occasions, like when you didn't kill?"

"When I had the impulse to do something, maybe I didn't go through with it because maybe I had worked overtime, or had other plans that I didn't want to back out of, afraid that if I did someone would say he didn't show up for this or that. Working overtime meant less daylight time to go out and try to find a boy or something. Sometimes masturbation worked."

"When you told us about telling Lee that you were going to have to kill him in the morning, had you already come to some decision at that time about what you were going to have to do to him?" asked Jensen.

"Yeah. I had to go to work and I knew I had to show up and I couldn't just leave him there. He was a bright kid, he could identify me. So to kill him was the only thing I could do."

"Did you consider maybe you could drive him back to Portland, or anything like that?" asked Jensen.

"I had thought about it," said Dodd. "And I thought maybe I could drop him off somewhere near the playground where I found him or something, that somebody would see him and get him home right away on account of the conditions and everything. But, um, I decided, you know, it was too big of a risk going back into that area."

"Too much of a chance to get caught?"

"Yeah. Too much."

"When did you decide that you had to stab Billy and Cole?" asked Sundby.

"While I was doing the oral on Cole. I knew, you know, that they'd tell. And with my record. . . . The boys were shook up enough that the parents would know something was wrong, and they'd find out what happened and then the boys could identify me."

"Had you planned on that when you went into the park?" asked Sundby.

"I thought it was a possibility that I might have to kill. I was hoping I'd go in and maybe find a boy that was willing and would cooperate, and then I'd just let him go and nothing would probably be said. I guess I was kind of ready for anything when I went in there."

"Did you ever go back to David Douglas Park after killing the Neer brothers?" asked Sundby.

"No."

"Did you ever go back to Vancouver Lake?" asked Trimble.

"No."

"Did you ever consider turning yourself in?" asked Trimble.

"Yeah, I have."

"Why?"

"There were a couple articles written about Lee. He talked about the mail lady, and in the article she had said how nice Lee was. I read that she said he was a special kid on her route, and that hit me kind of hard and I thought about going to the Vancouver police then. A newspaper columnist wrote something, I don't remember who it was now, but he said something about 'watch the beast' at the end of the column. I think reading those articles was when I started feeling guilty about it and I thought a couple of times about going in."

"Are you glad it stopped tonight?" asked Jensen.

"Yeah."

When the interview was over, Jensen, Trimble and Sundby couldn't wait to get away from Dodd. They all agreed that their child killer had been caught, and they were happy about that. But each of the detectives had been sickened

240

and repulsed by Dodd's repugnant story. It was the worst case that any of them had ever been assigned, and they hoped they never had another one like it again. Despite a list of 160 sex offenders, each a possible suspect, Dodd's name hadn't been among them. Although relieved that Dodd was in custody, each of the detectives was also dismayed at how the system had failed everyone involved, especially the victims. Dodd's arrest had been nothing more than a lucky break, a fluke, and there could be no telling how many other victims Dodd would have claimed if he had not slipped up that night in Camas, Washington.

Chapter Fourteen

As with any investigation of great intensity, many things involving many different people happen simultaneously, and the homicide investigation of Westley Allan Dodd was no exception. Dodd was turned over to the Clark County Sheriff's Department and booked into that agency's jail facility during the early morning hours of Tuesday, November 14, shortly after he made his confession to Detectives Jensen, Trimble, and Sundby in Camas. During that same time frame, at 4:45 A.M., Detective Rick Buckner, accompanied by Deputy Jeff Smith and FBI Special Agent Michael Sanders, rousted Berniece Walker, Dodd's landlady, out of bed.

Buckner knocked loudly on the door to Walker's darkened house, located at 9816 Northeast Third Street in Vancouver. After a couple of minutes Buckner saw a light come on, after which a woman's voice asked, "Who is it?"

"Detective Buckner of the sheriff's office," said the detective. "I'd like to ask you a few questions about one of your tenants, Wes Dodd."

Buckner showed his identification to Walker

through the window, after which she opened the door and allowed him and his colleagues inside. Buckner explained the circumstances surrounding Dodd's arrest in Camas a few hours earlier, but made no mention of the fact that Dodd was also the focus of the Neer brothers and Lee Iseli murder investigations.

"He wouldn't do something like that," Walker said of the attempted kidnapping charges against Dodd. "Something is wrong."

"Can you tell us when Wes moved into the apartment?" asked Buckner. Walker pulled out her records and studied them for a few minutes before answering.

"He moved in on August thirtieth of this year," she said. She explained that the apartment rented for two hundred dollars a month, which included all utilities, and was furnished with a bed, chest of drawers, a rug, and a nightstand. She said that Dodd shared a kitchen and a bathroom with an adjoining apartment occupied by a man named Larry Barnes.*

"He paid his rent on time," she offered.

"Have you ever gone into Westley's room?" asked Buckner.

"Why, no," she replied. "The last time I went into his room was about two months ago."

"How many keys are there for Wes's apartment?" asked Buckner.

"There are two," she said. "He has one and I

243

have the other. Westley is such a nice boy, he helps me all the time. He doesn't use drugs, smoke cigarettes, or drink."

"Has he ever had any friends or visitors over?"

"No. He's never had any friends over to my knowledge. His father stopped over once. Actually, his father came over every now and then when the boy had car problems."

"Have you ever seen any boxes of papers or books in Westley's apartment?" Buckner was thinking of Dodd's diary, and was wondering about any pornography that might have been noticed by the landlady.

"He has some books," she said. "He likes to read a lot."

"What hours does he keep? You know, what time does he go to work, get home, go out, things like that."

"He normally leaves for work about seven o'clock in the morning," she said. "He gets home about four or four thirty in the afternoon, and usually stays in his room after that." She thought for a moment and then said, "For the past two weeks or so, he did go out quite a bit at night but he always came back around ten o'clock."

"Think back to the Sunday before Halloween," said Buckner. "Try to remember as much about that day as you can."

Walker said that she had left for church at approximately 10:00 A.M. and returned home

244

about 12:30 P.M. When she came home, she noticed that Dodd wasn't there, but he returned later that afternoon. She said that he left his apartment at another point, but returned again. She couldn't pinpoint the times, however, and seemed to be struggling with her memory about it. Naturally the detectives wondered just how accurate she had been regarding the time she returned home from church, but they never said anything. The first time he came home, she explained, she had been sitting by her front window when she saw Dodd drive up and park on the street. He then walked to his apartment, which he had to enter by going around the side of the house.

"Was there anybody with him?" asked Buckner.

"Not that I could see."

"Has Westley ever talked to you about where he eats his lunch?" probed Buckner. "Do you know if he ever goes out to Vancouver Lake with a sack lunch or anything like that?"

After a short pause she emphatically stated, "I know he wouldn't kill anybody!"

"I didn't say that he did," said Buckner.

"We're just trying to conduct an investigation," interjected Special Agent Sanders. "We never said that he had killed anyone." Sanders and Buckner brought the topic back to the Sunday prior to Halloween.

"How long was Wes gone when he left again in

the afternoon?" asked Buckner.

"He was gone long enough to, say, get some groceries," responded Walker. Again she was unable to be specific about the time he returned, but she said she thought it must have been around 1:30 P.M. or 2 P.M. She said that she hadn't noticed whether he had taken anything into the apartment with him when he returned, but he stayed only a short time and then left again. He returned home a short time later, stayed the rest of the afternoon, and left again at about 8:00 P.M.

"He was gone that time for about two hours," said Walker. "I was in bed when he returned, but I heard him when he came in."

"Have you ever heard any unusual noises coming from Westley's apartment?"

"No, can't say that I have. Other than the normal noises, like from the shower or when the toilet gets flushed."

"Have you ever heard a small child's voice coming from his apartment?"

"No."

"On that Sunday before Halloween, did you see Westley carry anything back and forth between his apartment and car? Anything at all?"

"No, not that I recall."

Buckner explained that he needed the only other key to Dodd's apartment besides the one Dodd was carrying with him when he was arrested. He said that he and his colleagues would be obtaining a search warrant for the apartment, and they didn't want anyone to go inside or disturb any of the contents prior to their serving the warrant. She provided him with the only other key.

"Can you please show us the entrance to Larry Barnes's apartment? We need to ask him some questions since his and Wes's apartments share a common kitchen and bathroom." Walker pointed to the door, and told them that he was probably still asleep like she had been.

When Barnes answered the door, obviously still half asleep, Buckner explained to him, like he had done with the landlady, why they were there.

"I'm glad it's just plain kidnap," said Barnes.

"What do you mean by that?" asked Buckner.

"Well, with all the weirdos out there, ya never know. I'm just shocked about Wes."

Barnes explained that he had lived in his apartment for approximately two months, and said that Dodd was already living in the other apartment before he moved in. He said that his first impression of Dodd was that there was something different about him. However, he said that he couldn't put his finger on what was different or strange about him.

"Have you ever seen anyone at Wes's apartment?" asked Buckner.

"No," said Barnes. He thought a moment and then added, "Actually, I saw a small boy there once, a couple of weeks ago. He was approximately eight or nine years old. He was watching TV, and Wes said that he was his sister's son."

"Do you know anything else about Wes?"

Barnes explained that Dodd told him that he had moved from Seattle, and that he'd had a small boy born out of wedlock. Following a bitter custodial dispute that Dodd had told him about, Dodd obtained custody of the child and shortly thereafter the boy died. Buckner raised his eyebrows slightly but said nothing about Barnes's last statement. Barnes added that Dodd kept a picture of the child in his room.

"Is it possible that Wes is homosexual?" Buckner's question came out quickly and had gotten Barnes's attention.

"I'm not a homosexual," Barnes quickly pointed out. Buckner said that he hadn't meant to imply that he was, but was merely wondering about Dodd's sexual orientation. Barnes said that he thought it was possible that Dodd was gay, but he didn't know that for certain.

When Buckner asked him about the Sunday before Halloween, Barnes explained that he had gone to church at 3:00 P.M. and returned about 6:00 P.M. He said that he had probably worked the day shift at Burgerville, a fast-food restaurant, before going to church.

"What about the child you saw in Wes's apartment? Can you tell us more about that?"

Barnes explained that he had seen the child at about eight o'clock in the evening. After hearing voices from the kitchen, he said he went over to Dodd's apartment and opened the door. Dodd told him that the boy was his sister's son, that he was eight or nine years old, and that he was staying overnight.

"Can you describe the boy?"

"He had blond hair, and was wearing one of Wes's T-shirts," said Barnes. "He was about four feet high."

"How do you know how old the boy was?" asked Buckner.

"That's what Wes told me. He said that he was that old, either eight or nine, I'm not sure which."

"How do you know the boy had on one of Wes's T-shirts?"

"Wes told me that the boy had spilled hot coffee on his shirt and that he had given him one of his to wear while the boy's dried."

Barnes seemed very nervous during the interview, and at 6:05 A.M. asked the detectives if he could be excused for a few moments so that he could say a prayer. Buckner told him to go ahead, and watched as Barnes walked into the kitchen where he knelt down and began to pray.

It seemed like a strange time to pray, until Buckner and his colleagues considered how the implications of their visit might affect someone who may have seen a child murder victim during the last hours of his life.

When he returned a few minutes later, he explained that he had heard voices coming from Dodd's apartment a few weeks before. He couldn't be specific about the date, but said that he thought it might have been on the same day that he'd seen the small boy in Dodd's room. Barnes said that the boy's blond hair was combed straight down on the sides and in front, and that he had seen him for only a short time, perhaps only fifteen minutes, before returning to his own apartment. Barnes said the child didn't appear to be frightened, and that he had seemed contented.

Buckner excused himself at 6:25 A.M. and walked outside to his car. Using the car phone he called Dodd's stepmother and asked if Dodd's sister, Kathy, had any small children who might fit the description of the child that Larry Barnes had just provided. She told Buckner that Kathy's only children were her stepchildren, and they were living with Kathy's husband's ex-wife. Dodd's stepmother told Buckner that she didn't believe Dodd had ever seen or met any of Kathy's stepchildren. And even if he had, Kathy or any other of Dodd's relatives certainly would not allow any children to spend the night with him.

Buckner returned to Barnes's apartment and informed him that he and Sanders needed to drive to the Camas Police Department to obtain a photograph that they wanted him to look at, and said that they would be gone only as long as it would take to make the trip and retrieve the photo.

It was 7:47 A.M. when Buckner and Sanders arrived back at Barnes's apartment. Sanders explained that they were going to show Barnes a photograph, but first they wanted him to think back to October when he saw the small boy in Dodd's apartment and to picture in his mind what the boy had looked like. After a few moments Sanders showed Barnes the photograph of Lee Iseli.

"Does this look like the boy you saw?" asked Sanders.

After about forty seconds Barnes responded. He said that the hair looked like the hair on the boy that he saw. He continued to look at the photo and, after about a minute had passed, he said, "Yes, that could be him but he looked older to me." He also pointed out that the boy he had seen had blue eyes like Lee Iseli's.

"Did you see whether the boy left with Wes the next morning after you saw him?" asked Buckner.

"No, I didn't," said Barnes. "I haven't seen the boy since that one day in October."

That same morning the investigators contacted officials at Dodd's place of employment, Pac Paper, where he had worked and was still officially employed as a shipping clerk. The owner of the company characterized Dodd as a model employee who was very conscientious about his work and had never missed a day since he started. Dodd had first been sent out by a temporary employment agency, and Pac Paper had put him to work packing adding machine paper rolls into boxes as they came off the machines. After a week and a half of that, one of the supervisors told Dodd that he liked his work and would hire him full time after he completed his obligation with the temporary agency. Approximately four or five days after Dodd went full time, he was promoted to the position of shipping clerk.

"He was the last person you would suspect," said an official of the company when told of the investigation and the attempted kidnapping charges against Dodd. "It's absolutely devastating. If you had a man who didn't miss a day of work, was willing to work weekends, was very sharp, articulate and diligent, what would you think? The supervisors here were looking for ways to promote him even further."

One official told Special Agent Sanders that Dodd was a very capable employee who got along well with the others. He said that Dodd was very punctual and had not been disciplined for any kind of disruptive behavior on the job. A review of the time cards showed that Dodd was off on October 29, but was back to work at 7:00 A.M. on October 30. Similarly, Dodd did not work on September 4, Labor Day, but reported for work at 6:45 A.M. on September 5.

One of Dodd's coworkers recalled that on one occasion, shortly after hearing about the Lee Iseli murder, she had commented to Dodd how despicable the crime was and elaborated about what type of scumbag person would commit such a horrendous crime. The coworker said that Dodd had not responded to her comments, and said that she would have expected a response if she had held the same conversation with other employees. Instead of responding to her, she said, Dodd just looked down and acted dejected.

Chapter Fifteen

No one could believe at first that Westley Allan Dodd had always been a monster, especially during his childhood. But as information and inquiries from police agencies throughout the state poured into Clark County, many began to believe it. Much of what came in were police and psychological reports that detailed an extensive history of sexual contact with children, some of which began while Dodd was still a child himself. If he hadn't always been a monster, many wondered, perverse from the womb so to speak, then what had he been?

By Dodd's own account, which he had freely given to a number of law officers and psychologists, he evolved slowly into a monster starting at about age thirteen. His behavior had seemed innocent enough when it all began, he said, when he was "just flashing and touching," but he gradually progressed to the point where, by age twenty-five, he began entertaining thoughts of rape and murder.

Dodd was born on July 3, 1961, in Toppenish, Washington, the oldest of three children. He was eleven months old when his brother, Greg, was born, and in time he grew to resent his parents for the attention they showed to the new addition to the family. Matters only got worse when Dodd's sister, Kathy, was born when he was four. By that time, he said, he was all but forgotten by his mother and father.

"I remember after getting out of jail in '83 or '84," said Dodd, "when my dad told me that I just crawled off to a corner and played by myself when my brother was born. And that was fine with them. I was occupying myself and they had time to spend with the baby. That's kind of the way it's been ever since. Why? I don't know."

In 1964 his family moved to Kennewick, Washington, one of the Tri-Cities, where Dodd attended grade school until age eight. During those early years Dodd's father worked mostly for dairies making route deliveries, and his mother, while primarily a homemaker, worked occasionally as a cook for restaurants around town.

Dodd's earliest memory of his parents was when he was six or seven years old. He had been playing in the backyard of their house in Kennewick and was talking to some neighbor kids over the fence. At one point he climbed up on the fence so that he could better see who he was talking to.

"I was up on the fence and I fell off," recalled Dodd. "The next thing I knew I was lying on my back up by the back porch. Apparently one of the neighbor kids had dragged me up there after I fell off the fence and passed out. So I went inside and told dad. I was scared, thought I was gonna die or something. I had never passed out before. Instead of hearing what I wanted to hear, which was, 'Are you going to be okay? You're not going to die,' I was sent to my room and punished for being up on the fence. Dad didn't care that I was hurt. All he cared about was that I'd broken a rule."

Dodd said that by the time he was ten years old he heard his parents arguing nearly every night while he listened from his bedroom. He described his parents' relationship as "lousy," and said that "they fought all the time. They were vicious, they fought over dumb things." He said that although the family went camping and picnicking together, his parents argued constantly during the outings. He reported that there was no affection, no love shown in the family. "There was no love there at all, we were never close at all," said Dodd.

Dodd said that his father doled out the discipline in the family. He said that his father was very forceful and stated that he grew up fearing him.

"I felt he didn't care about me at all," said Dodd. "Up until the time my parents got a divorce, I did everything I could to avoid dad. I guess he always took his anger out on the first available person or object. If me or my brother or sister did one little thing wrong, something really minor, all hell would break loose.

"When somebody did something wrong, Dad would listen to the first story, and that was it. That first story was the right one in his eyes. It didn't matter who told it, but it was usually my brother or sister. I guess it was because I was the oldest, I was supposed to know better. Even when one of them had started a fight, it was my fault because I was the oldest. Things just seemed real unfair. And looking back on it now, I'd have to say the same thing."

It is important to note that later, following the murders and Dodd's arrest, his siblings refuted his statements about there being no love in the family.

Dodd reported to a therapist that he had felt relieved when his mother and father separated. He had known that a divorce was imminent, and he was happy when it finally happened. By then the family had moved to Richland, Washington, another of the Tri-Cities. Their lives, he said, were marked by frequent moves within the city and constant problems between his parents.

"I realized that they weren't going to tell us about the divorce," said Dodd. "We overheard them talking about it, and that's when they decided they'd better tell us. I didn't know it at the time, but when I think back about it that's something that really makes me angry. It was about two or three days before my fifteenth birthday when they told us about it. My brother and sister cried about it, but I didn't. I remember feeling guilty about it. Psychologists say that it's normal, that kids often think that the divorce of parents is the kid's fault.

But that's not why I felt guilty. I felt guilty because I was glad they were getting a divorce. I didn't think it was right to be feeling that way. You're not supposed to feel that way, people say. But the arguing and fighting would be over.

"My dad likes to play God," said Dodd. "He likes to play mind games with people. If somebody doesn't see things his way he convinces them that they're wrong. He convinces them that they have the problem and he tells them how they can fix it. Which in the long run makes him happy. He doesn't care about how anyone else feels. I noticed that really coming out with my stepmom. He married her a while back, and I see him doing that to her all the time."

Dodd recalled that his mother remarried when he was sixteen or seventeen, and he had disapproved of her choice for a new husband.

Dodd attended Columbia High School in Richland, where he graduated in 1979 with a 3.0 grade point average. Dodd said that his grades were better in high school than they had been in elementary school, due in part to improved peer relationships. He still hadn't formed any long-term friendships, but rather just got along with kids better. Dodd "never did any good at sports," but was above average in music and drama. The only academic subject he did poorly in was "government class," which he hated. But he got along well with his teachers, most of whom, particularly his music and drama teachers, seemed to like him.

Dodd described himself as being a very shy person, someone who didn't like to talk in front of a group of people. However, that fear changed when he signed up for drama in high school. He found that he liked drama and the attention it brought him. As a result he took drama classes for two years. Despite having been drawn out of his shell somewhat, Dodd remained shy with people when he had to deal with them on a one-to-one basis. For that reason, he said, he did not date girls in high school.

"I feared women, they made me nervous," said Dodd. "Even though I liked some girls, I never tried to approach them. I didn't have a whole lot of friends. I had one date in high school, and I originally tried to get out of it. But I went ahead and went on it. It was one of those dates where the girls ask the guys out, a Sadie Hawkins dance or some such thing. I didn't know how to act around girls, didn't know what to do."

Dodd began working when he was fourteen, and held a part-time job throughout his high school years. When pressed about why he didn't have any friends, he stated that he didn't have much time for friends. He said that in addition to his jobs there were band rehearsals after school, and the band was required to travel with the football and basketball teams. Dodd said that he had been drunk only one time in his life, and smoked marijuana on only one occasion. He skipped class only one time, and "felt very guilty about that." In short, he said, he just never got involved with the other kids and never did the things that they did.

"Kids that I'd meet at school for the first time," said Dodd, "would ask me, 'You don't do drugs, do ya? You don't drink beer, do ya?' They could tell by looking at me that I wasn't involved with anything like that. In fact, girls used to tease me quite a bit. They would tell me that my epidermis was showing, and I would look down and see if my fly was open. I didn't know at the time that epidermis was my skin. Later the girls used to call me 'clean cut and handsome,' and that would embarrass me. I didn't like it then, but now I'd love to hear that. People just seemed to think that I would never do anything wrong. And in a way, I think, that kind of bothered me. Everybody thought I was so perfect and *couldn't* do anything wrong. I later thought, well, 'I could be just as bad as the rest of them.' "

By the time he was fourteen, simple flashing was no longer enough to bring about the thrill he desired. When asked what caused him to progress to more serious types of criminal behavior, as opposed to remaining in the mindset of just exposing himself, Dodd said that it was to achieve the same level of sexual thrill.

Dodd described instances that occurred during the summer of 1976 in which he had stripped off all of his clothes and walked nude down public bicycle trails in the Tri-Cities. He also often sat on logs and masturbated while naked. On one such occasion an older girl stumbled upon him, and he ran away from her, hoping that she wouldn't be able to describe him adequately to the police. It was also common for him to ride his bicycle in the nude along the trails, and "skinny dipping" became a frequent event.

At age fifteen, according to what he told a psychologist in 1987, Dodd found himself alone with an eight-year-old boy on one occasion. He took the boy into the bathroom, they removed their clothes, and he tied a string around both of their penises to "attach" them. Dodd then laid on the floor, and coaxed the boy to lay on top of him. A short while later, Dodd got into a kneeling position and told the boy to try and penetrate his anus. The boy was unable to do so, but urinated on him instead. By the time he turned sixteen, his urge to "see male nudity" escalated dramatically, and he began coaxing young boys into sexual activity with him.

At another point, when Dodd was reported to the police for sexually abusing a five-year-old boy and a six-year-old girl, he was placed in therapy. "We didn't talk about anything," he said, and he was eventually placed into group therapy with other children. He learned about sexual intercourse at that time and "what homosexuals did," but quit the group after two sessions. As would later be the rule, he found that he could not discuss his problem in front of others.

Prior to the group therapy sessions, Dodd had not been taught about sex by anyone and did not know the names, even the slang and vulgar terms, for male and female genitalia. Female genitalia was simply known as "kee-kaw" to him, a term he had learned from the young girls he'd played a sexual "game" with at a playground. A psychologist theorized that Dodd's lack of sexual knowledge was likely due to the fact that he received no parental sexual education about the "birds and the bees," at least that's what Dodd had told him, and because he was a loner. If he would have made friends his own age, they would have helped him to mature both sexually and emotionally. But he had no such relationships during his lifetime, which likely contributed to the childlike ways that followed him into adulthood. It was as if children were the only people he could relate to, and some believed that if he had made one good, close adult friend in his life it might have precluded him from escalating his behavior to rape and murder.

But any such bonding and friendship were nonexistent in Dodd's life, and by age seventeen he was continuing, even broadening, his pattern of predatory behavior. He told a psychologist that he continued to stalk kids on the bicycle paths, and reported several more instances of molesting young boys.

Despite numerous complaints that were called in to the police about Dodd's sexual contact with children during his teenage years, nobody was willing to press charges against him. Most of the files still existed, but the outcome of most of the cases was unclear.

"Everybody decided that it wasn't bad enough to do anything about," said Dodd. "The police were ignoring me, my parents were ignoring me. The police asked me about several incidents around town, and I said, 'Yes, those were me.' And they said, 'Well, we're not gonna press charges.' Looking back I can see that, in a way, I was taught by the police that it was okay to do that. I don't blame them for anything, but they decided there wasn't anything bad enough that anything needed to be done. And I think that was the wrong way for them to think."

Even with psychiatric counseling or treatment, including behavior modification, Dodd was aware that his desires and impulses to expose and molest would always be there, as would be the lust and the fantasy. Although intensive and long-term treatment might have taught him how to keep these aberrant desires and impulses under control, it would not have eliminated them.

"I think you're probably right," Dodd had said. "About all you could do is learn how to control it. All the counselors and psychologists that I've talked to have said that. 'That's all we can do is teach you how to control it.' It's like alcohol or drug addiction. It's something you've got to stay away from for the rest of your life. . . . There is no cure for it."

At age nineteen Dodd joined the U.S. Navy, in part to avoid having child molestation charges brought against him. Of course the Navy knew nothing of his background in pedophilia or they wouldn't have allowed him to enlist. But because of Dodd's uncontrollable drive to continue molesting children (there was never any attraction to adult males), the Navy would find out about his problem within two years and kick him out.

At first Dodd satiated his unnatural desires by fantasizing about former victims and masturbating at least twice weekly, particularly while he underwent submarine training in Groton, Connecticut. However, masturbation and fantasy soon were no longer enough. After he was stationed in Bangor, Washington, he began hanging around arcades where he frequently propositioned seven- to ten-year-old boys. In one incident, he said, "I talked the little boy into contact, took his pants down and had him stand on a toilet while I masturbated him and did oral sex on him." He had the boy masturbate him, too, and placed his fingers in the child's anus.

Once, when Dodd was on liberty, he encountered a lone eight-year-old boy. Dodd paid the boy one dollar to coax him into watching Dodd push an ink pen filler down his own penis. He paid the child another dollar to pull his pants down, after which Dodd placed his mouth on the boy's penis.

In another instance Dodd went "looking for another boy, saw a five year old and a three year old," both of whom went with him. He gave the boys money to take their clothes off, after which he orally sodomized them. He again placed the ink filler in his own penis, and performed oral sex on one of the boys again. Dodd returned the three year old to where he had found him, but continued to fondle the older child. He soon heard the five-year-old boy's father calling him, and saw that he was accompanied by the police. Dodd fled the scene, but was eventually arrested and given a general discharge from the Navy.

Following his discharge from the Navy for his sex-related offenses, Dodd moved back to Richland where he lived with his mother and worked as a dishwasher for two weeks. He soon was in trouble with the law again after propositioning and fondling a five-year-old boy. He was arrested and was in and out of counseling a number of times due to a court-ordered mental health treatment plan in connection with the incident. At one point he served twenty-three days in jail for failing to meet the conditions of his court-ordered treatment plan, and upon his release he moved to Idaho. While in Idaho he lived with his father for one year, and held jobs at a convenience store and a Taco Time restaurant. When his employers found out about his record of child molestations, he was fired.

After moving to Lewiston Dodd met a nine-year-old boy and his single mother. He befriended them, and after they got to know each other better he began baby-sitting the boy on weekends. On one weekend in particular the boy's mother went out of town, and she had asked Dodd to take care of the child for her.

"On a Saturday morning," explained Dodd, "he was taking a bath. We were gonna do some things that day, and he was getting ready to go. But he forgot to take a towel into the bathroom and he asked me to bring him one. I really loved the kid, I didn't want to do anything to hurt him. I made conscious efforts that I wasn't going to molest this boy, I don't want to do that. His own dad never did anything with him, didn't want to be around him. When the boy had problems, he'd come to me. But that morning he wanted me to bring him a towel, and I asked him if he wanted me to bring it in or leave it by the door. And he told me to bring it in."

Dodd described how he took the towel into the

bathroom and left it on top of the toilet seat. When he turned to walk away, the boy asked him to stay and keep him company.

"So I started thinking," said Dodd, "well, he doesn't mind if I see him without any clothes on. That night he wanted a back rub, and I gave him a back rub. I guess by that point I had decided I was going to molest him. I wasn't sure what his reaction would be if I asked him to pull his pants down or asked him if I could do different things. While I was rubbing his back I asked him if he wanted me to rub his legs, and he said that was okay. I patted his rear end and asked him if he wanted me to rub that, too, and he said if I wanted to I could. I asked him if he wanted me to rub it over his underwear or if he wanted me to take it off. He told me to go ahead and pull it off.

"I had my hand under his underpants," continued Dodd. "I pulled them back up and rubbed his chest. But I still wasn't *really* sure he would let me molest him. I wanted to do oral sex on him. I just wasn't sure what his reaction would be. I didn't want to do anything, I guess, to ruin the friendship that we had. I asked him if he wanted me to stay in there until after he fell asleep, and he said, 'Yeah,' that it would be okay. He wanted me to keep on rubbing his back. So I decided at that point that I'd wait until he fell asleep, I'd pull his underwear off, and molest him while he slept.

"He fell asleep, I kept rubbing his back and his legs, and kind of just worked his underpants off. I started doing oral sex on him while he slept. He started to stir a little. He was on his back and he turned over onto his stomach. I spread his legs apart a little bit, reached underneath him, and moved his penis back between his legs and started doing oral sex on him again that way, while he was on his stomach. I found out later on that he'd been having some problems with his mom and had been seeing a child psychologist, and that's when it all came out. Apparently, at the time he was lying on his stomach he woke up while I was doing oral on him. I was charged with lewd conduct, and was sentenced to ten years. It was commuted to a year in the county jail, and I ended up serving four months of it, in Lewiston's Nez Perce County Jail."

Following his release from jail, Dodd was ordered to continue treatment. According to Dodd, he spent a total of two years in therapy in an outpatient program for sexual offenders sponsored by the state of Idaho. Although a report sent to Richland authorities suggested that Dodd was making progress, there is no public record of whether he completed the program in Idaho.

In 1986 at the age of twenty-five, Dodd moved back to the Tri-Cities area. He rented an apartment in a complex that was inhabited mostly by single mothers, and began a five month "sexual relationship," as he called it, with a four-year-old boy who lived nearby after witnessing the boy and a three-year-old girl exposing their genitals to one another. After seeing the incident Dodd approached the kids and "threatened to tell" their mothers. Later, Dodd coaxed the boy back to his apartment where he fondled the boy.

The sexual contact became a ritual, approximately four times a week. Dodd and the victim's mother also engaged in sexual intercourse on one occasion. Dodd later told a therapist that he and the victim's mother "tried it once more, but we couldn't do it because we were in a hot tub." Shortly thereafter Dodd moved to Seattle, where he continued to masturbate to fantasies of his previous victims.

Following Dodd's conviction of attempted unlawful imprisonment in connection with the boy at the construction site in Seattle, clinical psychologist Kenneth L. Von Cleve supervised Dodd's treatment in a state-sponsored sex offenders' program. Von Cleve eventually made the following behavioral observations:

A mental status examination revealed a 26-year-old Caucasian male whose thought processes appeared to be clear and logical. Answers to questions were relevant and appropriately elaborated. Mr. Dodd does not appear to suffer from psychopathology; no looseness of associations were noted and ego boundaries appeared adequate. Similarly, no hallucinations or delusional thinking were reported. Mr. Dodd presents as being emotionally disturbed and as having a severe problem in the area of deviant arousal toward minor males. He was cordial and cooperative throughout the evaluation and no anger/hostility were noted. No suicidal/homicidal ideation was reported. Mr. Dodd appeared to be somewhat remorseful with regard to his assaults on minor males. However, he presented as having a limited concept of injury to his victims. Further, this individual presents as being alienated socially, and extremely immature emotionally.

In addition to interviewing Dodd at length, Von Cleve administered a series of standardized psychological tests that included the Minnesota Multiphasic Personality Inventory (MMPI) and the Multiphasic Sex Inventory. What follows is Von Cleve's assessment of Dodd based on Dodd's background, history, interviews, and test data:

Mr. Dodd's performance on the MMPI resulted in a profile of questionable validity. He is seen as being extremely naive. Although he did not present himself in an unusually favorable light, he responded to a number of items in a fashion that would indicate dishonesty. Mr. Dodd's profile clearly approximates that of other individuals who have been convicted of child molestation. It does not appear that this individual is at risk for chemical dependency.

Mr. Dodd's performance on the Multiphasic Sex Inventory, again, reflects an extremely naive and immature person. He does not appear to be sexually obsessed and was highly open about his sexual deviancy. Although cognitive distortions and immaturity were noted, these were not to an extent that would reflect a character disturbance or victim-like stance. Mr. Dodd's profile does not reflect a severe lack of accountability for his actions. He did not justify his sexual deviancy and would appear to accept accountability. At the present time, Mr. Dodd appears to be highly motivated for treatment.

Mr. Dodd's performance on the projectives, again, does not reflect psychopathology. Mr. Dodd's responses reflect immaturity and a limited concept of human emotions. Low self-esteem and feelings of unworthiness pervaded his responses. Mr. Dodd can be described as an individual who has had no intimate relationships with anyone over the course of his life. As such, he remains extremely emotionally immature and totally unable to function as an adult on an emotional level. His responses indicate a basic distrust of relationships. This likely accounts for his tendency to isolate himself and to stalk and assault young children who are safe and not in a position to reject him.

This individual's predatory pattern over the course of his life indicates significant deviant imprinting and suggests a pressing need for close monitoring. This is the most extensive history of predatory assaults on minor males I have had the occasion to record in an individual this age.

Von Cleve fashioned a treatment program for Dodd that consisted of "extensive aversive conditioning, very close monitoring, and ongoing behavioral assessment." The areas where Dodd needed the most help, said Von Cleve, were in controlling his deviant sexual arousal, learning appropriate sexual arousal, understanding the cyclic behavior of offending patterns, and correcting cognitive errors. He also needed assertiveness training, self-monitoring skills, education in dating etiquette and sexual approach skills, sex education, and victim personalization and empathy skills.

However, when Dodd's probation for the Seattle attempted unlawful imprisonment conviction expired in the fall of 1988, he promptly quit Von Cleve's treatment program despite the fact that program officials declared him far from being cured. He worked for a gas station/convenience store in Renton for several months, where nearly everyone reported liking him and trusting him completely. At one point he left the job and went to work for a painting company, but soon came back to the gas station/convenience store because the painting job was "too physical."

In May 1989 Dodd moved to Buckley, a small town east of Tacoma, where he worked for another gas station. In July his former girlfriend with whom he'd had a very short-lived relationship showed up with a child that she claimed was his, and they left for Yakima where they stayed for five days in a motel until she left him. Broke and alone Dodd moved to Vancouver, and shortly thereafter the murders began.

Chapter Sixteen

While his colleagues were conducting interviews with Dodd's landlady, neighbor, and employer, Detective Dave Trimble spent much of Tuesday, November 14, sprinting between his office and the Clark County Prosecutor's office as he put together an affidavit of probable cause for issuance of a search warrant. At 5:30 P.M. Trimble presented the affidavit before Clark County District Court Judge Robert Moilanen inside the judge's chambers. Moilanen read over the document, then signed warrants authorizing the searches of Dodd's apartment and his car.

Trimble and Jensen arrived at Berniece Walker's residence at 6:50 P.M. They were met there by Detective Sergeant Bob Rayburn, Detective Randy O'Toole, who is Clark County's evidence officer, and Dave Schmierbach and Randall Wampler, technicians from the Oregon State Police Crime Laboratory. On the advice of Deputy Prosecutor Roger Bennett, the lawmen asked Mrs. Walker and her tenant, Larry Barnes, to sign consent to search forms which allowed them to search common areas shared at the residence with Dodd. A few minutes later they served the search warrant on Dodd's apartment. It seemed silly to do so, knowing that Dodd was in jail, but they followed procedure and knocked on the door to Dodd's apartment and then entered with the key they had obtained from Walker earlier when no one answered. At that point the scene was turned over to Detective O'Toole, and technicians Schmierbach and Wampler.

Prior to anyone entering the apartment, O'Toole made a video recording of the exterior of the residence. Similarly, upon entering, O'Toole videotaped the interior prior to the collection of any evidence. Dodd's apartment, noted O'Toole, was very clean, neat, and orderly. It seemed like he had a place for everything, and everything seemed like it was in its place.

A three-shelf bookcase filled with a set of encyclopedias and a variety of other books sat near one corner adjacent to the bed. On the bottom shelf was a pile of recent newspapers, very neatly stacked, and on top of the bookcase was a thirteen-inch television. Next to the bookcase was a small writing desk that was pushed up flush with the wall. There were two alarm clocks inside the spaces on the headboard, and a drawing of a Nazi swastika in the middle.

Near the bed against another wall sat a chest of drawers, and in its bottom drawer O'Toole found a number of ropes and belts that conceivably could have been used as restraining devices. In another location O'Toole found a set of X-Acto knives, still in their case.

In addition to the aforementioned items, among the other objects seized as evidence from Dodd's apartment were bed sheets, plastic from around the bed's box springs, a sleeping bag from the center closet, a garbage bag and three blankets, and a wooden shelf bearing as yet unknown stains from the closet. After dismantling the bed and seizing the headboard and footboard, both of which had strands of rope attached to each side, they found what would soon be referred to as "the thing" beneath the bed, Dodd's briefcase. They photographed it just as they found it, retrieved it but did not open it at the scene.

During the search they also found a rectangular wooden device bearing ropes at each corner, and they would later learn, after reading Dodd's diary, that the device was to be used as a "torture rack." They also seized a package of garbage bags, a roll of undeveloped but exposed 35mm film, several volumes of "parent-child" books, and a copy of the New Testament, still in its original box. When he flipped through it, O'Toole found where someone had written "Satan Lives" on one of its pages. On the facing page someone had written profanities, and on another page there was a scrawled passage that described Satan as a "Love-God."

In their search for hair, fiber, and other trace evidence, O'Toole and the crime lab technicians removed the apartment's rug and took a number of vacuum sweepings from the floor, closet, and other locations. At one point they found a box of jeans, from which they located and removed a number of hairs. They also seized a rubber foot mat outside the apartment door, and collected the ashes from the outdoor burn barrel.

Afterward, Tommy Ray Moorefield and Michael Thomas of the Identification Division of the FBI's Washington D.C. laboratory processed Dodd's apartment for latent fingerprints. Similarly, Special Agents Joe Dezinno and Wayne Oaks from the Hairs and Fibers Section of the same FBI lab processed Dodd's Pinto station wagon for serological evidence as well as hair and fiber. They noted that Dodd's car was in such a poor state of disrepair that he had used duct tape to keep the rear doors closed.

Finally, at the medical facility of the Clark County Jail, a search warrant was served on Dodd's person. Two vials of blood were subsequently collected from Dodd, as were strands of his head and pubic hairs.

In the meantime, Detectives Jensen, Trimble,

and O'Toole met at the Clark County Sheriff's Office where they opened "the thing," Dodd's briefcase. Inside, a pair of neatly folded boy's "Real Ghostbusters" underpants nearly jumped out at them. They were identical to a pair that Jensen and Trimble had obtained from Lee Iseli's father for purposes of comparison. They knew that killers such as Dodd typically kept such personal belongings of their victims as "trophies" so they could relive the experience of the murder through fantasy.

They also found several manila envelopes, each of which contained handwritten documents that they assumed made up the diary or journal that Dodd had spoken about during his confession. They were meticulously organized and labeled "Incident 1," "Incident 2," and "Incident 3." They also found an envelope that contained most, if not all, of the news clippings about the murders of the Neer brothers and Lee Iseli. As they read through portions of the diary, they could feel their hatred for Dodd rising with each word.

It was a vile and disgusting journal kept for the sole purpose of reliving the experiences of his child molestations and, they would later read, murders, just like keeping the underpants had been. But with all of the dates, times, and explicit descriptions of what he had done to his victims, it was more than just a souvenir. It was incriminating as hell, and they knew that the diary would literally seal Dodd's fate when the case came to trial if it was admitted as evidence.

The most unsettling piece of evidence found inside the briefcase, however, was the pink photo album labeled "Family Memories." The photos inside depicted Dodd engaging in deviant sexual acts with Lee Iseli, both before and after the child's death, as well as nude photos of Dodd in a sexually excited state. The most horrible pictures, of course, were those of Lee Iseli after death, particularly the one that showed him hanging from a rope inside Dodd's closet. The photos made the seasoned cops' emotions run high as each felt varying degrees of anger, sadness, hatred and revulsion. The photos were so repugnant that they made the detectives feel like they needed to vomit.

A short time later, after Clark County Prosecutor Art Curtis reviewed the evidence and Dodd's confession to police, Dodd was charged with three counts of aggravated first-degree murder in connection with the deaths of the three boys. Curtis made it clear that he would seek the death penalty, and would try the case in two separate trials. One trial would be for the murder of Lee Iseli, and the other for the murders of William and Cole Neer. That way, said Curtis, he would have two shots at getting the death penalty for Dodd.

Dodd was also charged with one count each of first-degree attempted kidnapping and first-degree attempted murder in the New Liberty Theater case involving Steve Hall. The next morning at 9:00 A.M., despite his detailed confession to the detectives, Dodd pleaded "not guilty" to all of the charges after Vancouver attorney Lee Dane was appointed to represent him.

Although it would take a month or more to get the results of all of the evidence submitted to the FBI, the Oregon State Police and Washington State Patrol crime labs, the detectives would eventually positively confirm that Lee Iseli had been inside Dodd's apartment. In all, sixty-eight items were examined for trace evidence according to the Locard Exchange Principle which states that "objects, surfaces or persons which come into contact always exchange trace evidence." Some of the items examined would place Dodd and Lee Iseli together.

A hair found on Dodd's bed sheets was found to be consistent with hair standards taken from Lee Iseli's head. Similarly, stains on the wooden shelf, seized from Dodd's closet, were examined and confirmed to be of the same blood type as Lee Iseli. But the most conclusive physical evidence placing Lee Iseli inside Dodd's apartment, aside from the photos in Dodd's album and his confession, turned out to be a fingerprint lifted from a stapler found inside Dodd's desk drawer, and two toe prints and one footprint lifted from a piece of sheetrock near the overhead storage compartment of the closet inside Dodd's apartment. Each of these prints was compared with prints obtained from Lee Iseli's body and was confirmed by the FBI as Lee's.

Meanwhile Dodd's photo, as well as one of his car, was flashed across television screens all over Oregon and Washington, and appeared in virtually every major newspaper up and down the West Coast. As a result, numerous people began calling in with information related to the case. Most called to report sightings of Dodd and his car in the area of Richmond School on the day Lee Iseli was abducted. Portland Detective Dave Rubey took many of the calls.

One man who lived in the area of Richmond School remembered driving westbound on Southeast Caruthers Street the day Lee was kidnapped. As he passed by Forty-first Avenue, he saw a yellow Ford Pinto station wagon with Washington plates parked near the school. He said there was nobody in the car when he drove past, but recalled seeing several children playing in the school yard at the time.

Also, a woman called in to report that she had

seen a person that closely resembled Westley Allan Dodd at the Fred Meyer store located at Southeast Thirty-ninth Avenue and Hawthorne Boulevard three or four days before Lee was abducted. The man, she said, followed her and her two young children around the store's variety section for approximately twenty-five minutes. After seeing Dodd's photograph in the newspaper, the woman said she was certain that he was the same man.

Similarly, another woman reported that she had seen Dodd on September 23, 1989, at the Montavilla Community Fair held in Portland's Montavilla Park. She said that Dodd had spoken only to young boys at the fair, and had taken a number of Polaroid photos of the children. She said that she not only felt that his behavior regarding the picture taking was strange, but felt that his attire was inappropriate for the weather. It had been a very warm day and the person she believed was Dodd had been wearing an army field jacket.

Another woman remembered seeing Dodd's car on October 29 between 2:00 P.M. and 3:00 P.M., parked on Southeast Forty-second Avenue between Southeast Lincoln and Division Streets, near Richmond School. There was nobody in or near the car, however.

Rubey also spoke to a woman who had previously talked to a detective shortly after Lee Iseli disappeared. But at that time Dodd had not yet been apprehended, there were no suspects, and she had not reported seeing a yellow Pinto station wagon circling the blocks around Richmond School between 11:30 A.M. and noon on October 29. But now, after having seen Dodd's picture and a photo of his car in the newspaper, she felt that she should report the incident. She said she saw the car circle the school at least two times, but had not paid any attention to the driver. However, she said she saw a person that looked like Dodd in the school playground either before or after she saw the car circling the blocks. The person she had seen walked directly through the playground, but she said that she did not see him approach any children.

During this same time frame a neighbor of Dodd's reported to the police that she recalled observing Dodd arrive home with a small blond boy about the time that Lee Iseli disappeared.

"I thought nothing of it at the time," said the neighbor. She described the child as being no more than five or six years old, and wearing a lightweight jacket. "My feelings are asking me now if this was the little Iseli child . . . I don't even want to think about it," she said.

Another woman, a resident of Washougal, Washington, which is located near Camas, reported that she and her husband had taken their children to the 9:00 P.M. showing of *Honey, I Shrunk the Kids,* at the New Liberty Theater on Sunday, November 12, the evening before Dodd tried to abduct Steve Hall. There were very few people in the theater that evening, she recalled, and she and her family sat in the middle of the theater. Dodd, she said, sat several rows behind them and to their right, near the exit next to the restrooms. She was adamant that the man she had seen was Dodd after seeing his photo in the newspaper. The woman said that she had glanced back occasionally at Dodd throughout the movie and saw him watching her children. When they left the theater following the movie, Dodd followed them very closely. She said that after they got inside their car, they watched Dodd get inside a "funny" colored yellow Pinto station wagon that was parked near their car. She had gotten a very good look at the man that evening, she said, and was certain that it was Dodd.

A man living in the 3700 block of Southeast Lincoln Street reported that he saw Dodd drive his station wagon slowly past his house at least twice near the date and time that Lee Iseli was believed abducted. The man stated that he has an excellent memory, and could recall that the Pinto was mustard yellow with woodgrain sides. He further stated that he remembered that it had Washington license plates, the first three numbers of which were 288. Rubey recalled that the license plate on Dodd's car was 288-CIU.

A Vancouver woman reported that she may have seen Dodd near Vancouver Lake Park on the day before Halloween, October 30, at approximately 7:30 P.M. The woman had just left the Humane Society on Fourth Plain Boulevard and was proceeding east toward Fruit Valley Road. Just before she got to Weigel Street, an older, small station wagon with wood paneling turned west onto Fourth Plain from Weigel. The thing that had grabbed her attention was the fact that the station wagon's driver had failed to turn on his headlights. She flashed her lights at the driver to alert him, yet he still did not turn on his headlights. She only noticed one person inside the car, but she could not identify him. One of the task force detectives noted that it is possible to come from La Frambois Road, then turn onto Fourth Plain by taking a back road just off Weigel Avenue. Given the date, time, and location, the woman had likely seen Westley Allan Dodd right after he had disposed of Lee Iseli's body near Vancouver Lake.

With all of the reported sightings that police felt certain actually involved Dodd, such as all of the aforementioned, there were just as many, probably more, in which Dodd couldn't have been involved. The latter reports came from all over Portland and Vancouver, and from as far away as Camas to the east and Kelso, Washington, to the north. But when the investigators checked the dates and times of those reported sightings, they found that Dodd had been at work in most of the incidents.

Because of the high volume of inquiries that began coming in from other law enforcement agencies across the region shortly after Dodd's arrest, Clark County Sheriff's Department Sex Crimes Detective Sharon Krause was assigned to respond to the queries and to make follow-up contacts.

Detective Krause was informed by Detective Buckner that the task force had established that the first name of Dodd's ex-girlfriend was Anna, and that she was possibly living in Forest Grove, Oregon. Krause called her colleague in Forest Grove, Detective Aaron Ashbaugh, and asked if he could check around for her. Krause had a phone number for Anna, which she gave to Ashbaugh.

A few hours later Ashbaugh called back. He had identified the subject as Anna Hauge,* 27, the woman who had lived with Dodd in a Yakima motel for a short time in July. Ashbaugh said that he had talked to her at her residence, and she was very emotionally upset and had difficulty talking at times.

Ashbaugh said that Hauge told him of how she had met Dodd in Renton, Washington in July, 1988. She had moved in with him for a short time and later, after she moved away, gave birth to a boy that she believed had been fathered by Dodd. The boy, who she named Ryan, was currently living in a foster home at an unknown location in Washington State. When she and Dodd got together again in July, 1989, they moved to Yakima. When she was ready to leave him again, he made the statement, "I'll get even."

Hauge indicated that during the time that she had known Dodd, she was never aware of him abusing any type of drug or alcohol. She also said that Dodd had told her about his "problems with young boys," but that he had never exhibited any type of sexual misconduct with her or her children from previous relationships. She said that she felt Dodd had been a good father figure to her sons, and that he had often cared for them when she was not at home or when she was sleeping.

Hauge said that to her knowledge Dodd had never been in the Forest Grove area, nor did she believe that he knew she was currently living there. Ashbaugh said that she had told him that Dodd reportedly had taken nude photographs of one of his former roommates' infant sons. The former roommate, Wayne Nolin,* had told her about the incident involving his son.

As the task force detectives carefully studied Dodd's background, it became increasingly apparent that he fit many of the characteristics outlined in Dr. Turco's profile. Turco's profile, which was modeled after the classic serial killer profile developed in the 1970s by Special Agent John E. Douglas of the FBI's Behavioral Sciences Unit at Quantico, Virginia, was so chillingly accurate that it made the readers' blood run cold. They realized that the murders Dodd had committed were sexually motivated and that all of his crimes were ritualistic. Each of his crimes was repeated in a definite observable pattern, which thus formed the ritual. His pattern, aside from the method of murder, rarely digressed from crime to crime. His ritualistic behavior, simply put, provided the framework in which his darkest fantasies could be played out, and in some dark way he was able to justify his actions to himself. They recalled that Cole Neer asked him, "Why are you doing this to us?" Dodd had replied, "Because I have to do it."

Chapter Seventeen

On December 6, 1989, Detective Dave Trimble led Detective Don Smith of the Benton County Sheriff's Office to an interview room inside the Clark County Jail. Smith was there to determine if there was any connection between Westley Allan Dodd and a young juvenile named Michael Knox. Knox, Smith told Buckner, disappeared from his Richland home on August 14, 1979, and it was shortly thereafter that Dodd, who had been a resident of Richland at that time, had enlisted in the U.S. Navy. Knox's skeletal remains, said Smith, were discovered in November, 1979.

Dodd was promptly brought into the interview room, where he took a seat at a round table across from Smith and Trimble. After he was Mirandized, Smith explained to Dodd that he was interested in clearing up any criminal cases that he may have been involved in within the city of Richland. Smith told Dodd that he knew all about Dodd's incidents of indecent exposure in Richland from 1979 to 1981 of which Dodd spoke freely, even about incidents that had not been reported to the police.

"Do you have any knowledge about the disappearance of Michael Knox?" asked Smith.

"No," replied Dodd. "I've never heard of him."

"Do you recognize this boy?" Smith handed Dodd a photograph of Michael Knox.

"No."

"If you had been involved in the disappearance of Michael Knox, would you tell me about it?" asked Smith.

"Sure, why not?" responded Dodd. "What's one more?"

"Yeah, that's what I thought, too."

Smith and Dodd continued discussing Dodd's time in Richland, and focused primarily on Dodd's problem with molesting children and exposing himself. At one point, Dodd changed the subject, without any prompting from Smith, and began talking about the killings of the Neer brothers and Lee Iseli. Smith didn't ask him any questions about those cases because he felt that it would have been inappropriate to do so, but he listened as Dodd spoke. Dodd eventually started talking about the feelings he had been experiencing after his arrest.

"What do you think they're going to do to you?" asked Smith at one point.

"Either life in prison or the death penalty," Dodd answered. "I hope I get the death penalty."

The next day, December 7, Dodd was scheduled to appear before Judge Robert Harris at 1:30 P.M., and jail officer Morey Braddock was assigned to transport him to the courtroom. As Braddock eyed Dodd's private cell from a distance, he noted that the light was off and he could not see Dodd inside the cell. When he approached the door and peered through the window, however, he observed Dodd lying on his mattress near the wall. He was masturbating through his coveralls. Braddock opened the door and ordered Dodd out, and told him to remain standing by the door as he relocked it. Dodd's erection, Braddock noted, even through his coveralls, was obvious. Dodd appeared normal despite having been caught masturbating, and did not seem to be embarrassed over the incident.

Although Detective Rick Buckner had followed up on Anna Hauge's information regarding Dodd's alleged molestation of Dodd's former roommate's young son, Mark Nolin*, it wasn't until Friday, January 5, 1990, that he knew the full story. Buckner was doing paperwork at his desk as one of the coldest winters on record raged outside when his phone suddenly rang at 3:00 P.M. It was Rita Laurent, a counselor at the Clark County Jail. She was presently with Westley Allan Dodd, and Dodd was asking to see Buckner.

"Should I come over to the jail?" asked Buckner. "Or should we bring Dodd down to my office?"

After a short pause, during which time Laurent asked Dodd what he wanted to see Buckner about, she came back on the line.

"He says it will be rather lengthy," she said. "So maybe you'll want to see him in your office." Buckner agreed.

"Is this about Mark Nolin?" asked Buckner when Dodd arrived at his office twenty minutes later.

"Yeah, it is." Dodd was quiet for a moment.

"You know, Wes, we tried to talk to you earlier in the week about Mark, but you indicated you wanted your attorney present. Do you still want your attorney here?"

"No, I want to talk to you."

Buckner took him through the procedure of Miranda again as a precautionary formality, and Dodd agreed to sign a waiver card. That in effect made Dodd's statement, in legalese, "initiation after invocation," meaning that Dodd had initiated contact with the authorities after earlier invoking his rights against self-incrimination.

"Okay," said Buckner, "why don't you go ahead?"

"I was living with my sister and brother-in-law up in Renton," said Dodd, "and my brother-in-law's relative came to stay with us and look for work. He had a little boy about two years old."

"What was the little boy's name?"

Dodd explained that the child's name was Mark Nolin, Wayne Nolin's child, and that they had moved in with Dodd and his relatives in March, 1987. Dodd helped Wayne get a job, and one day after Wayne and Mark had been there for about three weeks, Wayne had to go to work but couldn't find a baby-sitter. Since Dodd was off work that day, he volunteered to watch Mark for Wayne.

"I'd seen the boy takin' a bath and I'd changed his diapers a few times," said Dodd. "I'd thought a little bit about molesting him."

Dodd went on to describe how he fellated and had simulated intercourse with the infant. It was three months after the sexual attack on the baby that he had been arrested in Seattle for the attempted abduction. While he was in jail for that incident, Mark and his father moved to Sunnyside, Washington, but soon moved back in with Dodd's sister and brother-in-law. When Dodd was released from jail during the first week in November, he said, he moved back in with them at their apartment, located at 707 South Seventh Street in Renton. Just after Christmas, however, Dodd's sister and brother-in-law moved, leaving

Wayne and Mark there with Dodd. It was shortly after that, he said, that his molesting of Mark escalated.

"Was he able to speak yet, to say no?" asked Buckner.

"No," said Dodd. "He couldn't talk at all, at that time."

"Uh-huh." It was all Buckner could do to remain calm, unemotional.

For a few brief, fleeting moments Buckner recalled Dodd's photograph of Lee Iseli, when Lee was still alive, with his hands tied back over his head on Dodd's bed. It made him sick, but he had to listen. It was his job, and he wanted to do everything within his power to nail this sonofabitch. The creep had already hung himself with his diary, photographs, and confession, but Buckner knew that more was better than less, just in case some of the other items got thrown out at trial. So he listened as Dodd described many other incidents of his rape and bondage sessions with the two-year-old boy over a period of several months.

Before finishing up the interview, Dodd told Buckner about another incident involving a baby boy. This child was the youngest yet, about a year and a half old. Buckner thought he'd heard everything, but Dodd never ceased to disgust him.

Chapter Eighteen

At 10:46 A.M. on Thursday, January 25, Custody Officer Dave Winders of the Clark County Jail's Medical Section called Detective Rick Buckner's office and left a message that Dodd wanted to see him again. Buckner was out of the office all that day, however, and didn't receive the message until the following day.

What could Dodd want now? Buckner wondered as he read the message. Not another confession to sit through, he hoped. Dodd's sessions with Buckner had been enlightening to be sure, but they had also been repugnant, sickening to a "normal" person, really nothing more than opportunities for Dodd to relive his prior crimes against his helpless victims. Buckner didn't think he could stomach another meeting, but he knew he had to find out what Dodd wanted to see him about. It was 4:47 P.M. when he showed up at Dodd's private cell in the medical facility, where he was being kept isolated from the other prisoners for his own protection. Every cellblock in the jail had asked that Dodd be placed in with the other prisoners because "they want to hurt him."

"Can you deliver this?" Dodd asked Buckner as he handed the detective an unsealed envelope.

"What's this?" asked Buckner as he opened the letter. He saw that it was addressed to the Prosecutor's Office. He read the following, written in Dodd's own hand:

Mr. Prosecutor,   1-25-90
My lawyer says I can't do this, but I'm going to try anyway. He's not let me make any of my own decisions. He told me he could do things over my objection if necessary. I wish to change my plea to GUILTY on ALL COUNTS. I have asked Detective Buckner to deliver this to you. I know of no other way to get around my attorneys. If this is possible to do, please ask for whatever hearing is required.
(signed)
Westley A. Dodd

When Buckner finished reading the letter, he looked quizzically at Dodd.

"Are you sure you want to do this, Wes?" asked Buckner.

"Yes." Dodd nodded his head.

"I want to make sure that this is your decision and no one else's," said Buckner.

"It is my decision alone," responded Dodd.

"It's so late in the day, Wes, and there's probably nobody over in the Prosecutor's Office at this time. I'll pass this on to them on Monday. I don't know if you can even plead guilty to first-degree aggravated murder, but I'll find out and let you know on Monday." Buckner took the letter and placed it into evidence.

Dodd made his desire to plead guilty known at a time when the state of Washington was in an uproar regarding sex offenders living within its boundaries. Another sex offender, Earl Kenneth Shriner, forty, was just going to trial in Bellingham on charges that he had raped, choked, and mutilated an eight-year-old boy on May 20, 1989, a few months before Dodd had committed his crimes. The boy, who miraculously survived, was found naked and bloody in a wooded area near his home with his penis cut off. Despite the fact that Shriner, who had a twenty-four-year history of molestation and sex crimes charges on his record, was soon convicted and sentenced to 131.5 years in prison, a group calling itself "The Tennis Shoe Brigade" was vehemently lobbying the state legislature to adopt tougher laws to deal with sex criminals in Washington. Shriner's and Dodd's crimes and the efforts of "The Tennis Shoe Brigade" moved

Governor Booth Gardner into action with the formation of a twenty-four-member Governor's Task Force on Community Protection.

As a result, lawmakers in Washington created and passed a package of statutes in 1990 that required, among other provisions, for all convicted sex offenders to register with the police no matter where they moved within the state after completing their sentence; for authorities to publicize the release of recently paroled sex felons into a community; victim and witness notification whenever an offender with whom they were involved is released; longer sentences for sex offenders; a curb on early releases and work-release programs; more money to fund treatment programs for victims and offenders; and a civil commitment provision, perhaps the most controversial of the package, in which a repeat offender can remain locked up even after they have served their sentence if it is found that they pose a high risk of offending again. In all, the state estimated that the program would cost taxpayers one hundred million dollars a year. It eventually passed, and would be the nation's toughest set of laws in dealing with sex offenders.

In passing the legislation, many had argued that if such a package had been in force years earlier Westley Allan Dodd likely would not have been freely roaming the streets in search of new victims after having been caught for his earlier offenses. Dodd, apparently, was among those in favor of certain aspects of the anti-crime package.

Unknown to Buckner or Dodd's defense attorneys, Dodd had mailed the following letter to Governor Booth Gardner's office in Olympia the same day that he had given Buckner the letter to pass on to the prosecutor, prior to the enactment of the new legislation:

1-25-90

I'm sure you've heard of me. I hope this letter reaches you. My name is Westley Allan Dodd. I'm writing to give you my point of view on the citizen-written measure for sex crimes.

I agree with longer, stiffer sentences, and with a legal procedure to commit violent offenders through civil proceedings. I also agree with registering with county sheriffs. I also believe more money is needed for treatment of victims and offenders. The only thing I have a problem with, but do not totally disagree with, is warning the community when an offender is in their midst. While I believe the people have a right to know when an offender is in their community—it must be done carefully—it could create some dangerous situations.

For instance, if everyone knows where an offender lives, it could cause even more trouble. The offender would undoubtedly be harassed, making him/her more likely to re-offend. Also, "vigilantes" and other self-proclaimed "do-gooders" may decide to take matters into their own hands to make sure the offender does not re-offend. This could lead to all types of unwanted harassment by both sides, fights, property damage, physical injury to either side, or worse.

I mean this letter to be used to help stop others as myself. Also, do not forget about the juvenile offenders. I started when I was 13- or 14-years-old. By the time I graduated from high school, I'd been caught 5 times, and reported to police only 3 times.

I could have been stopped over 10 years ago, but each of those times no charges were filed. I was taught by the police that I could molest children and get away with it. When, much later, charges *were* filed, I did only 3 weeks in jail! I later committed 3 very violent offenses (ending with murders), while I should have been only half way through a 10 year prison term in Idaho (of which I served only 4 months).

Please, sir, I'd like an opportunity to tell you many things that could have stopped me. Maybe it could be used to stop other sex-offenders (both violent and non-violent). I also know what each child I molested could have done to prevent or stop my actions against them. It would be very easy to teach them what to do. Any child old enough to talk is old enough to learn what to do.

It's too late for me. Others can be stopped, and some *may* safely return to society. They need your help. Most of all, the kids need your help. If you would like to hear what else I have to say, please contact me. I'll answer any questions I can—either by mail, phone, in person—whatever. Let's use what I know to protect, instead of hurt, other children. I expect to receive the death penalty. Learn from me while you can.

Thank you.

(signed)

Westley A. Dodd

Lee Dane and Michael Foister, Dodd's defense team, were furious when they were informed what he had done. How did he expect them to provide adequate representation if he was going to go behind their backs and offer to plead guilty? They convinced him to withdraw his offer, for the time being.

A few days later Dodd's demeanor began to change. No longer as talkative, he seemed to have withdrawn and appeared depressed. During a security check on February 10 at 1:50 A.M. by a corrections officer, Dodd was observed standing next to the toilet, leaning against the wall. His head was resting in his hands, and he was crying very hard. His face was also very red, which indicated that he had been crying for a long period of time.

"What's wrong, Wes?" asked the guard. Dodd didn't respond immediately. After several moments he answered.

"I keep thinking about the kids," he said, then began crying again. As an added precaution Dodd was placed on a "suicide watch," in which a corrections officer would check his cell every few minutes.

Dodd subsequently told his mental health counselor that he had contemplated suicide several times but had changed his mind because he felt that he owed it to the victims' families to go through the judicial process. He said that he didn't want to take the "chicken" way out and deprive the victims' families their right to see justice carried out. When asked what he felt should happen to him because of the crimes he had committed, he thought for a moment and then said, "I should be executed."

In April it was brought to Detective Dave Trimble's attention that a female inmate, Mardi Harmon,* twenty-three, had written letters to Dodd and had received responses. When Trimble contacted Harmon and asked her why she had decided to write to Dodd, she responded that some of the women in her pod of the jail simply wanted someone to write to Dodd to see whether he would write back and, if he did, what he would say. She said that she had been "elected" by her fellow inmates to write the letter, and she had asked him "why he did it." She turned over to Trimble two letters that she had received from Dodd:

4-10-90

(Mardi), Hi! I just got your letter. You said you "just have to know what kind of person" I am, and that "there is good in everyone." Well, I don't know what kind of person I am any more, to tell you the truth, and there was once some good in me.

I used to stop and help whenever I saw someone broken down on the highway. I stood by some friends and was there for both when they divorced. Before I started molesting children, I was a real friend to many. I rented a room from a single mother once. The kid's dad was never around. I sat up late at night more than once with her 9-year-old son. He often cried himself to sleep because his own dad wouldn't visit him. I would have done anything for that boy, and he knew it — he wanted to call *me* dad.

Other kids that knew me looked up to me and trusted me. They all seemed to like me. Then I started to change. Instead of being their friend, I started molesting them.

You asked "why did you do this?" I don't know why — I wish I did. Five years ago I would have put my own life on the line for any child, for any reason. Just last year I had an alcoholic roommate. I saved his 4-year-old son from many beatings while he was drunk.

I never wanted to hurt anyone in any way. Now 3 boys are dead. I don't know why.

You asked if I'd found God. Yes — about 3 months ago. I was having trouble believing I could be forgiven for what I'd done. Several people reassured me I was already forgiven. I also feel I don't *deserve* to be forgiven — I don't deserve what God offers to all who ask in the name of Jesus.

I guess I have these doubts because I

know I can't forgive myself. I just don't understand how I could care about kids so much, and yet, do all I've done to some of them. Something made me change. I wish I knew what.

You said you think I'm very nice-looking. Thank you. Tell me what you look like so I'll know who to smile at next time you're in Medical.

Like you, my life growing up was no fun. I hate my dad and have no feelings either way for my mom. I'm not even sure where she lives.

I've only had one girlfriend I was ever serious about. She became pregnant and left me. We tried to work things out, but just couldn't do it. She said she left because she didn't know how to tell me she was pregnant.

We were together for two weeks when my son was 4-months-old. She left saying I'd never see my son again. My attorneys can't even find her now. Some say that may be what triggered my actions here in Vancouver—knowing I'd never see my son again. I don't know—I don't think that's it.

My son is 13 months old now. I'd give anything for all of this to have never happened, and to be able to be with Ryan now. In the two weeks I had with him, when he started to cry, I always got him to smile instead. I would have spoiled him rotten! I pray his mother finds a good man to help raise him.

Thanks for your letter. I hope mine doesn't bore you too much. If you still want to be my friend, please write.

Wes

The second letter, written a week later:

4-17-90

(Mardi),

You were surprised I wrote you back. I was surprised you wrote to me to begin with. I have trouble believing anyone would want to.

I hope you can get yourself off heroin, and stay clean. Do it for yourself, and for your daughters. Be good to yourself—you deserve it.

I was never molested, but was abused in many other ways (physically, verbally, emotionally, and often neglected).

You're right about needing a friend. The only thing I have to look forward to is letters from my friends, and there are very few of them.

You asked how old I am. I'm 28. I'll be 29 on July 3rd.

How much time did you get for your probation violation? You asked in your first letter if I'd found God. I have. The Gideons have been a big help. They are making sure someone sees me every Wednesday and Sunday. If you're not already talking to them, please do. They're a wonderful group of people. You can get some Bible study workbooks from them that have taught me a great deal.

A friend told me something she once heard a pastor say, concerning the sacrifice that was made for us: "I can think of many people I'd die for, but I can't think of one I'd sacrifice my only child for." That really makes you realize just what a sacrifice it was.

Well, sorry. I hope I don't sound like I'm preaching. It's just that I've experienced a peace I've never known before accepting Jesus, and I just want others to feel it also.

I look forward to hearing from you again.

Wes

The letters were quite a departure from Dodd's "diary of death," and he had seemed sincere in what he had written. But Trimble and others who would read them couldn't help but wonder if Dodd's religious conversion was for real. Anything was possible, he guessed, as he entered the letters into evidence.

Dodd's latest writing, however, wasn't limited to letters, as the authorities and residents of Washington and Oregon would soon find out. Throughout the month of May, Dodd talked about writing something that might help kids protect themselves from people like himself. Being cut off from the general jail population, Dodd told the jailers that would listen that he felt it was important for people to know how to protect their children from sex offenders and murderers. He seemed to relate particularly to the Camas incident, in which Steve Hall's unwillingness to cooperate had saved his life. Dodd wrote on and off, whenever the mood seemed to strike and whenever he wasn't masturbating in his jail cell. Finally, toward the end of May he mailed a document to *The Columbian* newspaper in Vancouver. It was titled:

WHEN YOU MEET A STRANGER
by
Westley A. Dodd

Introduction—written by a professional—who I am, what I've done, why this was written. There *are* things that *work* that kids *can* do to protect themselves. I have never molested or harmed any child that resisted me. Sometimes it took just a "no," sometimes it took more.

WHAT DO YOU DO?

Many boys and girls are told "don't take candy from strangers," or "don't get in a stranger's car." But what should you do when you're alone, and someone you don't know wants you to go with him, or wants you to pull down your pants, or do something else you know is bad? What do you do if there is no grown-up around that can help you? Do you do what the stranger wants, and hope he'll go away soon? NO!

The stranger is bigger and stronger than you, and you might be scared, but *you* can make *him* run away! Sometimes the stranger is just as scared as you are. He's afraid you might do something to get him caught. He'll leave you alone and run away from you.

How can a boy or girl make a grown-up run away when he wants to do something bad to you? *What do you do?*

JUST SAY NO!

You may have been told "just say no" to drugs. You can also say *no* to someone who wants you to go somewhere with him. You can say *no* to a person who tells you to pull down your pants, or take your clothes off.

There are other people like me. We make you take your clothes off. Some of us tell you to get in our cars. We can be nice to you, or we can be very mean. Sometimes, some of us want to hurt, or even kill you. But you can still get away.

A boy said *no*. Then, before I could say or do anything else, he ran away! I ran away too—I went the other way. I didn't want anyone to see me chasing him, and I was afraid he'd send the police back to get me. Say *NO!*, then *RUN!*

YELL! SCREAM!

Okay. You said *no,* but he held you so you *couldn't run,* or he caught you when you did run. Now what? Do you let the stranger do what he wants to you and hope it won't hurt? NO!

Another boy said no, then tried to run. I grabbed his arm and wouldn't let him go. He finally pulled his pants down and let me touch him, so I'd let him go. Is there anything else he could have done to protect himself? What?

I met another boy—he was 6-years-old. I told him, "You have to come with me." He said NO and tried to get away from me, but I picked him up and started to carry him away. He knew he couldn't get away, but he didn't give up. He started screaming and yelled, "Someone help me—he's killing me!"

He kept screaming and yelling for help. I was afraid someone would hear him, so I let him go and ran away. I didn't want to get caught, but the boy ran and told someone what happened and the police caught me ten minutes later. That 6-year-old boy didn't know what I was going to do. He only knew I was trying to take him away, and something real bad could happen. Instead of being scared and going with me, he yelled for help! He's a hero now because even though he was afraid of me, he screamed and yelled for help when he needed it.

Just say NO! Then RUN! SCREAM—it will scare him away! YELL for HELP! Get away fast and tell someone what happened! Always tell someone! Be a HERO!

Dodd's pamphlet was published in the newspaper right after Judge Robert Harris ruled that Dodd's confession to the police had been obtained legally, only days before his trial was scheduled to begin. Needless to say it outraged many, particularly his attorneys and those who thought his motive for writing it was self-serving. Many felt that he might have written the pamphlet to gain sympathy, while others thought that he may have been trying to make it even more difficult than it already was to seat a jury. Dodd, however, countered by saying that he was sincere when he wrote the piece.

"I'm just trying to show that, like I said before, I know from experience that these things do work," he said. "It's too late for me. Maybe someone else can be helped. I've got to do all I can in the time I've got left."

Chapter Nineteen

Despite the ardent objections of his defense team, Westley Allan Dodd requested and was granted a hearing before Clark County Superior Court Judge Robert Harris. On Monday, June 11, 1990, Dodd stood before the judge and announced that he wanted to change his pleas from innocent to guilty. In low monotones and with his head lowered, he confessed his crimes in court.

"On September 4, 1989, I went to David Douglas Park with the premeditated intent to cause the death of a human being," said Dodd, reading from a prepared statement. "I met Cole Neer. I raped Cole Neer and then I killed him. I also at about the same time murdered William Neer."

Dodd told Harris that he took a knife with him to the park with the intent of raping and murdering a child, and that he committed the murders to conceal his identity from the police. After killing the Neer brothers, he said, he felt a sense of fear but soon overcame it.

"I was nervous," he stated. "I was kind of afraid that I was going to get caught. And then as I watched the papers I realized that the police didn't have any clues. I started feeling a little bit more confident and realized I could do it and get away with it. The next step would be to actually kidnap a boy.

"On October 29, 1989," he continued, "I kidnapped Lee Iseli from Portland and drove him to my apartment in Vancouver. I raped him, and on the morning of October 30, I murdered Lee Iseli."

"Did you premeditate the killing?" asked Harris. "Or did you commit it on the spur of the moment, in a moment of haste?"

"No, sir," Dodd responded. "It was premeditated."

Dodd also admitted that when he attempted to kidnap Steve Hall from the Camas theater, it had also been his intention to rape and then murder the boy.

"Do you realize that you can be sentenced to death for crimes of aggravated first-degree murder?" asked Harris.

"Yes, sir."

"Are you going against the advice of counsel in changing your plea from innocent to guilty?" asked Harris.

"Yes, sir, I am," replied Dodd. "I want to plead guilty on all counts."

Prosecutor Art Curtis said that he was willing to accept Dodd's guilty pleas, but emphasized that Dodd's decision to change his plea was one that he made on his own without receiving any promises from the Prosecutor's Office.

"We've given nothing up," said Curtis. "He pleaded guilty to what he was charged with." Curtis said that despite Dodd's change of plea, he was still prepared to seek the death penalty.

Although Dodd's admission of guilt made it unnecessary for the state to continue with a trial on the issue of guilt or innocence, it would still be necessary to impanel a jury to decide whether Dodd should be sentenced to death or to life in prison, the only two sentencing options available for someone convicted of aggravated first-degree murder. By pleading guilty, Dodd relinquished the right to appeal many of the legal issues in the case, including whether the warrants used to search his apartment and car were legal and whether the confessions he made to police were valid.

The following month, after a jury of six men and six women were seated, Chief Deputy Prosecutor Roger Bennett began his presentation of the case. After telling the jury that they were there not to decide Dodd's guilt or innocence but rather whether he would be executed or spend the rest of his life behind bars, Bennett took the jurors step by step through the case, from Dodd's lurid past through the killings to his confessions. He showed them grisly photographs of the victims, and a twenty-minute video made by the police of the scene when Lee Iseli's body was found.

But perhaps the most chilling part of the more than two weeks of proceedings was that which focused on Dodd's diary, which outlined the killings in graphic detail as well as his future plans to kill children, the pact he made with Satan in which he described the devil as a "Love God" and prayed to Satan to help him achieve his murderous goals of selecting "The Chosen Ones." Bennett contended that Dodd's handwritten diary showed that he "planned to engage in a large number of long-term kidnapping and murders of young children." Bennett argued that Dodd's writings showed a desire to "torture children before he killed them." One diary entry, he said, described how he inserted a plastic tube into little Lee Iseli's penis which, contrary to Dodd's diary, the prosecutor said, must have caused excruciating pain for the child to endure.

Bennett produced schematic drawings from Dodd's diary that depicted a rack which he could use to tie up and immobilize his victims so that he could perform "experimental surgery" and dismember the children while they were still alive. Bennett's descriptions of Dodd's plans to surgically remove parts of the children's sex organs while they were conscious brought gasps from the gallery. Dodd's diary, said Bennett, told of numerous ways in which he could murder children. Some he planned to strangle, others suffocate. Still others would be drowned or poisoned. Dodd referred to the planned deaths, said Bennett, as his "experiments."

Bennett showed the jurors a map of David Douglas Park, drawn by Dodd, and an entry in his diary exclaiming that the park would be a "good place for rape and murder, or kidnap, rape and murder . . . a good hunting ground." He also pointed out how Dodd had written in his diary that he "got more of a high out of the killing than the molesting."

"Cole and William Neer died in David Douglas Park on Labor Day as victims of 'the hunt,' " said Prosecutor Art Curtis, his voice often cracking with emotion. "At least twenty other children avoided death through fate that weekend alone. Do you wonder where those children are? Who are the lucky ones?

"Lee Iseli met a friend at the playground, a nice man who wanted to buy him a toy, wanted to give him some money," continued Curtis. "Lee Iseli did what we teach our children not to do

. . . little did he know as he played happily at Mr. Dodd's apartment the night before his death that Mr. Dodd was sitting, writing in his diary."

Curtis then read a passage from the diary: "Six-thirty P.M. Lee is still playing. Will probably wait until morning to kill him. He suspects nothing now. That way his body will still be fairly fresh for experiments after work."

Arguing against leniency, Curtis told jurors there was no evidence for them to consider that warranted compassion or forgiveness for Dodd.

"Must I remind you of the crimes?" he asked. "How do you describe the enormity of the crimes for which the defendant has pled guilty—what is the appropriate word? Outrageous? Appalling? Beyond belief? Horrific? It is difficult to believe a human being is capable of fantasizing about such crimes."

"Look at what Mr. Dodd likes to do in his free time," co-prosecutor Bennett told the jurors as he reminded the panel that Dodd's one hobby and passion in life was killing. "Plan child murders. Commit child murders. Relive fantasies about child murders and write about them. With life without parole, two of those things are still available to him." Bennett urged the jury to sentence Dodd to death.

Dodd's attorney, Lee Dane, who is an opponent of the death penalty, argued that Dodd should be sentenced to life without parole. Dane said that Dodd would not pose a future threat to society because he kills only children, and none would be available to him if sentenced to life in prison.

"I'd like you to think about the effect of an execution on a community—whether it heals or hurts a community," said Dane. "The death penalty has never brought back a human life, has never elevated a community or the people who comprise it."

On Saturday, July 15, 1990, following fourteen hours of grueling deliberations over three days, the jury concluded after failing to find any mitigating circumstances or reasons for leniency, that Westley Allan Dodd must die for his crimes

Two days later Dodd granted an interview with Portland's KOIN-TV anchorman Mike Donahue in which he indicated that he would ask that his sentence of death be carried out as expeditiously as possible. He also said that he would choose hanging over lethal injection as the method of execution. Washington state is one of three states that still has hanging as a means of execution on its books.

"Last month just about every night I started thinking about those boys," Dodd told Donahue. "I'd cry about it. But then later in the night, I'd find myself thinking about what else I might have done with Lee Iseli or what would have happened had I got that other boy from Camas home . . . I don't want to sit there on Death Row thinking about those things."

Why did he want to hang?

"The main reason is because that's the way Lee Iseli died," said Dodd.

On July 26, 1990, Judge Robert Harris formally sentenced Dodd to death and he was promptly transferred to the Intensive Management Unit, where Death Row is housed, at Washington State Penitentiary in Walla Walla.

In the aftermath of his sentence, Dodd vowed that he would not appeal. But two lawyers, opponents of the death penalty, filed notice of appeal without his permission. The following January, Dodd wrote to the Washington State Supreme Court and asked that he be allowed to waive his appeals, making him the only Death Row inmate in Washington history to decline to appeal his sentence. Although the state Supreme Court upheld Dodd's trial and sentence, it ordered a hearing on Dodd's mental competency, to be held before Superior Court Judge Robert Harris, and allowed Dodd to file a brief to argue his case.

In the meantime, with the assistance of his new attorney, Darrell Lee, Dodd filed the brief with the Washington State Supreme Court asking that he be allowed to waive all appeals. In the brief,

Dodd argued that he should be executed as soon as possible. Dodd told the justices that those who were trying to save him from the gallows were trying to blame his crimes on society when he was trying to accept total blame and punishment for his deeds. Dodd said to the justices:

> Did the system fail? I have said all along the system does not work. The "system" did not commit hundreds of sex crimes against nearly 100 children. The system did not kill three little boys. I did. Is there mitigating evidence in my case? No. Do I feel remorse? No.
>
> If this case is sent back to a trial court, I will plead guilty again and physically and vocally demand my conviction and death sentence. I must be executed before I have an opportunity to escape or kill someone within the prison. If I do escape, I promise you I will kill and rape and enjoy every minute of it.

While the higher court considered Dodd's argument, Dodd appeared at the competency hearing on June 5, 1991, before Judge Harris. He had been examined by another court-appointed psychiatrist, who reported that he felt Dodd was competent to make his own decision on whether to file appeals or not. Dodd told Harris that he still thought about the murders and had sexual fantasies about the killings all the time.

"I don't want to think about what I've done anymore," said Dodd.

"Do you know what would happen to you (if you were allowed to waive the appeals)?" asked his attorney.

"I'm going to walk up the gallows," he replied stoically. "They put a black sack over my head and a rope around my neck and push a button."

"And what happens then?" asked Lee.

"One of two things," answered Dodd. "My neck snaps and I'm dead, or I hang there until I'm dead."

"You want that tonight?"

"Yes . . . all of these years they have gone to any length to arrest me and accuse me of all kinds of things, only to drop the charges or lessen the sentence and eventually let me go. Finally, they have got me on three murders; I have been found guilty and sentenced to death. I can't understand why, when I have gone along wanting to be executed, so much time and so many people have tried to find a way to let me loose."

Afterward, Judge Harris ruled that Dodd was mentally competent and understood the severity of his decision. As a result, no one would be allowed to file an appeal on Dodd's behalf without his consent.

On October 8, 1992, the Washington Supreme Court finally ruled that Dodd could waive all appeals. Nearly eight weeks later, on November 30, Dodd was brought back to Clark County one last time to appear before Judge Harris. Dodd, appearing gaunt and thin with sunken eyes, stood before Harris.

"Do you understand that if you don't start doing something you're going to be executed within the next few weeks or months?" asked Dodd's attorney.

"Yes," replied Dodd.

Judge Harris then set January 5, 1993, as Dodd's date with the hangman. Dodd was promptly returned to Walla Walla.

Meanwhile, Washington State Penitentiary officials went to work sprucing up the gallows, which hadn't been used since 1963 when a man named Chester Self was executed for the murder of a Seattle cabdriver during a holdup that netted only two dollars. They painted the walls, and the old mechanical levers that dropped the trapdoors were replaced by electronic buttons. Workers even washed the windows through which witnesses would watch the hanging.

On Monday, December 7, prison officials purchased the rope to be used in the hanging, as well as a black hood. The rope, made of Manila hemp, was one and one quarter inches in diameter. Prison employees boiled it and stretched it to remove any stiffness and to ensure that its "spring" would no longer pose a problem when Dodd dropped through the trapdoor. The last thing they wanted was to have his body bobbing up and down in front of the witnesses due to any elasticity left in the rope. The rope was also oiled and waxed to enable the knot to slip smoothly as it pulled taut around Dodd's neck from the weight of his 139-pound body. Finally, they brought in a carpenter who constructed a wooden collapse board, a device which could be strapped to Dodd's back to keep him upright in the event that he collapsed or became uncooperative when ordered to take his place on top of the trapdoor. If everything went off as planned, Westley Allan Dodd would be the first person to be executed by hanging in the U.S. since 1965. By then it was all up to Dodd.

Throughout the remainder of 1992, several attempts were made to halt the hanging. If no one could file an appeal on Dodd's behalf, then they would try to have Dodd's death warrant invalidated. One group, the Washington Association of Churches, asked Governor Booth Gardner to grant clemency to Dodd, but Gardner, who "was sickened" by Dodd's crimes, refused to intervene.

"I have read the court documents and reviewed

the circumstances of Westley Dodd's crimes," said Gardner. "It is my intention to let the death sentence be carried out."

On December 29, 1992, the American Civil Liberties Union and twenty-six taxpayers filed suit in Olympia, arguing that tax dollars should not be spent to kill someone by hanging, which they considered a "cruel and unusual punishment." The lawsuit did not challenge the constitutionality of the state's death penalty law, only that tax dollars should not be spent in hanging a man to death.

The following day Thurston County Superior Court Judge Richard Strophy ruled against the ACLU, which filed an immediate appeal with the state Supreme Court. On the afternoon of January 4, 1993, when Dodd had less than twelve hours to live, the Washington Supreme Court refused to halt Dodd's hanging. It became apparent that Dodd would drop through the gallows shortly after midnight.

Chapter Twenty

A thick blanket of freshly fallen snow covered a vast area of flat farmland that makes up much of eastern Washington. The desolate wintry countryside surrounding Walla Walla seemed an appropriate setting for a confessed child killer to spend the final segment of his life, far removed from the Northwest's major population centers that he had loved to prowl so dearly.

Earlier that day Westley Allan Dodd granted a final interview with a reporter from a Kennewick television station during which he said that he had made the choice to be put to death because death was a more lenient sentence, at least in his case, than spending the rest of his life behind bars. He said that he chose hanging over lethal injection as the method of death because of guilt over what he had done.

"I don't believe I deserve anything better than those kids got," said Dodd. "Those kids didn't get a nice, neat painless easy death. Why should I? In my case, I knew I could get the death penalty if I was ever caught, but I didn't care. A lot of people won't believe me when I say that I am sorry for the things I've done, but that's something that I need to say.

"If I have confessed all my sins," he continued, "I believe what the Bible teaches: I'll go to Heaven. I have doubts, but I'd really like to believe that I would be able to go up to the three little boys and give them a hug and tell them how sorry I was and be able to love them with a real true love and have no desire to hurt them in any way. I know they're there already."

The scene outside the Washington State Penitentiary on the night of January 4, 1993, seemed almost surreal. Shrouded by the still falling snow and encased by a fierce arctic chill, the prison, although aglow from the light-reflecting snow and the illuminated walls and guard towers, remained an ominous sight on the edge of town where it seemed as if it was cordoned off from the rest of the world. A small group of anti-death penalty protesters, contained in their own designated fenced-off area near the prison's entrance, chanted and waved signs as they shivered in nature's deep freeze in a demonstration that would last only forty minutes. Despite their presence everything seemed orderly, however, perhaps because the evening had been so carefully orchestrated by prison officials. It was a night to be remembered. One of the nation's most hated men was about to become the first man in thirty years to be hanged there, and the countdown to his death had begun.

The prison parking area that was designated for the news media was filled nearly to capacity, mainly with vans and trucks bearing satellite link-up dishes from major network affiliates from all around the country. Most of the news hounds, some from as far away as New York, had arrived early, long before the official 9:00 P.M. entry time, and many actually seemed eager to get inside the prison's walls and out of the cold.

It was precisely at 9:00 P.M. when prison officials opened a small gate and began leading the throng of reporters and writers inside in groups of ten, the number that an administrator had deemed manageable. After climbing a long flight of stairs each group was led into a small, yellow "checkpoint" building, where other prison officials, one by one, crossed the names off the official list of those whose entry to the prison had been pre-approved. As part of the in-processing procedure, they took each person's driver's license and in return handed out a numbered placard made out of plastic that had to be clipped to their shirt or coat so that it always remained in plain view. The back of each person's left hand was also stamped in yellow with the letters "WSP." After being duly informed that a body search could occur at any time, a group of guards continued to lead the potential witnesses, still in groups of ten, into another building behind the prison's walls. This was the visitor's entrance.

After a short delay, each group was led down a cold, austere gray corridor and through several electronically controlled sliding steel doors, each of which was locked securely behind each group before the next door would be opened. Finally, the groups sporadically arrived in a large room that had been designated the media center, where twelve witnesses would be selected out of the media pool to view the execution. By then it was a few minutes past 10:00 P.M., and Dodd had less than two hours left to live.

During a briefing from Veltry Johnson, the Washington State Corrections Department's public information officer, the media pool was informed that Dodd had eaten salmon, scalloped potatoes, mixed vegetables, coleslaw, and lemonade as his last meal. Johnson also said that Dodd had been with a member of the clergy and his lawyer for much of the evening, but didn't provide details of the meeting.

"What will happen if the hanging doesn't go off as planned?" someone asked. "Is there a contingency plan? What if Mr. Dodd strangles?"

"Then he will strangle," said Johnson. "This is a hanging. That is what is happening this evening. We have confidence in our procedures."

After an explanation of the lottery procedure and strict rules about leaving their equipment behind, the twelve witnesses were selected by a lottery process, coordinated by the prison's administrative assistant, Jerry Davis. Those whose numbers Davis called were led immediately by a guard out through a door at the front of the room and into a holding room. When all twelve witnesses had been selected, they were escorted out of the building and into the prison exercise yard, through a locked gate and across the frozen snow-covered ground and, finally, into a square gray building where the gallows was housed.

At 11:55 P.M., after being subjected to a pat-down search, the group was escorted into a room facing the execution chamber, which was little more than a bi-level compartment separated by glass windows from the witness viewing area. Jewel Cornell, Lee Iseli's mother, and Clair Neer, Billy and Cole Neer's father, were already there, seated next to Darrell Lee, the attorney who helped Dodd get his death wish granted.

Seconds after midnight, Dodd was brought from his holding cell twenty paces away and led into the upper level of the gallows. Wearing a white T-shirt, gray prison shirt, jeans and sneakers, he appeared in front of the large picture window. When asked if he had any last words, he stepped boldly up to a microphone next to the window and said, "I was once asked by somebody, I don't remember who, if there was any way sex offenders could be stopped. I said no. I was wrong. I was wrong when I said there was no hope, no peace. There is hope. There is peace. I found both in the Lord, Jesus Christ. Look to the Lord and you will find peace."

When Dodd finished speaking, an opaque screen was drawn over the upper level windows to protect the anonymity of the executioners. A back light was then turned on which eerily silhouetted Dodd as he took his place over the trapdoor. The witnesses below could see the coils in the noose as one of the executioners, chewing gum, placed the dark hood over Dodd's head. The purpose of the hood was to protect the witnesses from seeing the grotesque facial contortions associated with hanging and strangulation. A second executioner then positioned the noose around Dodd's neck, and set the knot just behind his left ear. Dodd's hands were tied in front of him with leather straps, and his legs were similarly bound together at the ankles. Dodd appeared cooperative and didn't waver. He didn't need the wooden collapse board after all. He was ready to die.

Very little time had elapsed from the moment Dodd had finished his statement and had taken his place over the trapdoor. At a given signal one of the hangmen pressed a button, and without warning the trapdoor beneath Dodd's feet snapped open with a loud bang. It took less than a second for Dodd to drop seven feet one inch, the length of rope that one of the hangmen had calculated would be needed to break Dodd's neck based on his height of five feet nine inches and weight of 139 pounds.

It was 12:05 A.M. Dodd's body swung somewhat, and a slight movement could be seen in his abdomen, along with some in his hands. His legs, slightly bent, seemed to flex for a moment, and seconds later his body went limp. There was no squirming, no gurgling, and no twitching. It seemed to everyone present that Dodd died quickly. Dodd's body hung there in the lower level in full view of the witnesses for a little more than a minute before the warden, Tana Wood, closed off the screen. A doctor pronounced Dodd dead at 12:09 A.M., and his body was cut down.

An autopsy would determine that Dodd's neck did not break as the hangman had planned. Instead, torn nerves and ligaments had caused Dodd to lose consciousness quickly and he strangled to death, just like his last victim. His body was cremated and turned over to his family for a private memorial service.

Westley Allan Dodd was gone forever, as were his victims. Whether Dodd was sincere in his words of remorse toward the end will never be known.

Most importantly, if lessons are to be learned from this case, we must never forget about what happened to Billy and Cole Neer and Lee Iseli at the hands of Westley Allan Dodd. To lose sight of this man's violent rampage would mean that the untimely and senseless deaths of those beautiful little children would have been in vain. Even though positive steps are being taken to combat the horrific problem of child molestations, pedophilia, and murder, much work remains to be done. Meanwhile, until such time that predators like Dodd can be effectively removed from our midst, society *must* remain aware that there are other Westley Allan Dodds out there at this very moment, lurking in the shadows and waiting for just the right moment to strike. . . .

WALK ALONG THE BRINK OF FURY:

THE EDGE SERIES

Westerns By GEORGE G. GILMAN

HE'S THE LAST MAN YOU'D EVER
WANT TO MEET IN A DARK ALLEY . . .

THE EXECUTIONER

By DON PENDLETON

Available wherever paperbacks are sold, or order direct from the Publisher. Send cover price plus 50¢ per copy for mailing and handling to Pinnacle Books, Dept. 729, 475 Park Avenue South, New York, N.Y. 10016. Residents of New York and Tennessee must include sales tax. DO NOT SEND CASH. For a free Zebra/ Pinnacle catalog please write to the above address.

DEATH, DESTRUCTION, DEVASTATION, AND DOOM
EXPERIENCE THE ADVENTURE OF

THE DESTROYER SERIES

By WARREN MURPHY and RICHARD SAPIR

Available wherever paperbacks are sold, or order direct from the Publisher. Send cover price plus 50¢ per copy for mailing and handling to Pinnacle Books, Dept. 729, 475 Park Avenue South, New York, N.Y. 10016. Residents of New York and Tennessee must include sales tax. DO NOT SEND CASH. For a free Zebra/ Pinnacle catalog please write to the above address.